ISLAND  POKÉ

ISLAND  POKÉ

COOKBOOK

RECIPES FRESH FROM HAWAIIAN SHORES, FROM POKE BOWLS TO PACIFIC RIM FUSION

JAMES PORTER

Photography by Mowie Kay

RYLAND PETERS & SMALL
LONDON • NEW YORK

To Liv and the whole Island Poké family for making this possible.

Senior Designer Megan Smith
Commissioning Editor Alice Sambrook
Editor Gillian Haslam
Picture Researcher Christina Borsi
Art Director Leslie Harrington
Editorial Director Julia Charles
Production Manager Gordana Simakovic
Publisher Cindy Richards

Food Stylists Emily Kydd & Natalie Thomson
Props Stylists Tony Hutchinson & Alexander Breeze
Indexer Vanessa Bird

Published in 2018 by
Ryland Peters & Small
20–21 Jockey's Fields
London WC1R 4BW
and
341 East 116th Street
New York, NY 10029

www.rylandpeters.com

10 9 8 7 6 5 4 3 2 1

Text © James Porter 2018
Design and commissioned photography © Ryland Peters & Small 2018

ISBN 978-1-84975-968-7

A CIP record for this book is available from the British Library. US Library of Congress CIP data has been applied for.

Printed in China

NOTES
• Both British (Metric) and American (Imperial plus US cups) measurements are included in these recipes for your convenience. However it is important to work with one set of measurements and not alternate between the two within a recipe.
• All spoon measurements are level unless otherwise specified.
• Uncooked or partially cooked eggs should not be served to the very old, frail, young children, pregnant women or those with compromised immune systems.
• When following a recipe which uses raw fish or meat, always ensure you buy sashimi-quality ingredients and use on the day of purchase. Raw fish or meat should not be served to the very old, frail, young children, pregnant women or those with compromised immune systems, without medical advice.
• Ovens should be preheated to the specified temperatures. We recommend using an oven thermometer. If using a fan-assisted oven, adjust temperatures according to the manufacturer's instructions.
• When a recipe calls for the grated zest of citrus fruit, buy unwaxed fruit and wash well before using. If you can only find treated fruit, scrub well in warm soapy water before using.

FOOD SAFETY NOTICE
The information contained within this book is intended as a general guide to poke-making at home, based on the author's recipe development and experience. Although all reasonable care has been taken in the preparation of this book, neither the publishers nor the author can accept any liability for any consequence from the use thereof, or the information contained therein. Please consult an up-to-date government source on food safety for further information.

CONTENTS

INTRODUCTION

Let's first explain what poke is, and what it isn't.

A poke bowl is a healthy version of sushi, originating in Hawai'i. The Hawaiian term 'poke' translates as 'chop up in small pieces'. The dish can consist of any number of ingredients from the traditional 'ahi (or yellowfin tuna) to other fish, shellfish, octopus, tofu or seasonal vegetables. All these are marinated and served with Japanese- and Hawaiian-inspired sauces and condiments, such as kukui nuts and seaweed.

Although they say there are at least a hundred varieties in Hawai'i, poke has since morphed into almost unrecognisable variations since leaving its homeland. Despite not using traditional ingredients, some are generally true in spirit to what an islander would consider poke to be. Many more are full of unusual decorative and flavour touches, such as edible flowers, rice in shades of green and black, multiple fruit pickles and plenty of crispy kale.

As you'd expect, we have kept to the script with the more original Hawaiian combinations, which you'll find sitting comfortably alongside the more modern fusion versions of poke, both in this book and in our Island Poké stores. Not only scrupulously and correctly prepared with the best ingredients available, we keep to the 'island style' for that tasty, authentic, super-healthy vibe that captures the freshness and flavours of Hawai'i.

Island Poké started off on a tennis court in 2003. I was playing in a junior tennis tournament on Maui and actually won both the singles and doubles titles. It was a great moment for my tennis game, but in the long run something else overshadowed the tennis. This was what we were eating for lunch. The friendly local players seemed to be addicted to a cup of raw fish with two scoops of rice from the local Foodland supermarket. It may not have pushed them over the line in the tennis, but it certainly contributed to their Aloha spirit.

Fast forward to 2015. I left my job at Bonhams and started street trading in London. Although my tennis career lost its way sometime before I went to university, the lunch I remembered having in Maui formed the basis of my new venture. I tapped into that Hawaiian experience, and knew it would be great to share this little known dish called poke.

Since we moved into bricks and mortar in 2016, Island Poké has taken off as one of the main contributors to what has been described as 'poke-mania' in London. A lot of our success has to do with keeping things thoroughly 'island style'. This means poke that is uncomplicated, not overly embellished, and essentially familiar to anyone with experience in Hawai'i. Alongside the food, the 'island style' means a casual vibe, friendly service and staff who are dedicated to providing that aloha.

It is in this spirit that I examine the culinary roots from which the global poke phenomenon stemmed. One of the focal points is the range of traditional Hawaiian cooking that underpins the current scene on the islands. Locally these sorts of dishes are known as authentic 'ono grindz'. Another is fusion style, described as Hawaiian Regional or Pacific Rim cooking, a direct result of Hawai'i being practically in the centre of the Pacific Ocean. Finally, I look at how other countries around the world approach distinctive dishes on a parallel course as those Hawaiian originals.

We hope you think the passion for proper poke runs through from me, the founder, to the fabulous crew at Island Poké.

A big Mahalo, or thank you, to our friends and poke pals, and particularly to all those of you who are enthused by what's on these pages. I hope our enthusiasm will help cut you loose to try for yourself!

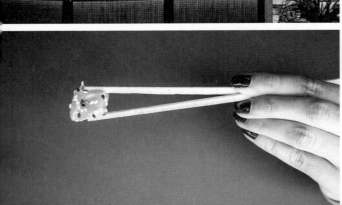

THE HAWAIIAN PANTRY

To get you started on your Hawaiian food journey, here is a little explanation of some of the more unusual ingredients used in these recipes – how to use them, where to find them and useful substitutes.

FURIKAKE a Japanese rice seasoning typically containing finely chopped nori seaweed, toasted sesame seeds, salt and sugar.

HAWAIIAN SEA SALT you can use normal rock sea salt as a substitute, just not iodized salt.

INARI WRAPS these are little Japanese parcels made using soya bean curd (similar to a sweet-ish omelette) wrapped around a combination of fillings, normally including rice as well as a couple of other ingredients, such as vegetables or raw seafood.

KAMABOKO this is similar to that imitation crab meat found in most grocery stores, also known as surimi. It's a Japanese fish cake made of compressed white fish. You can substitute imitation crab meat.

LŪ'AU LEAVES these are the large edible leaves from the taro plant. They contain a mild irritant so make sure you wash your hands after preparing (or use rubber gloves if you have sensitive skin) and always cook for at least an hour before eating.

LI HING MUI this is a dried, salted plum normally dyed bright red and frequently used in confectionery. The powder is often used to decorate cocktail rims or when pickling dried fruit.

MOCHIKO FLOUR this is a Japanese rice flour made from finely milled short grain rice. It gives a very light, slightly chewy texture. You could use normal rice flour or wheat flour as substitutes, although this would result in a slightly different consistency.

PITAYA POWDER this is a bright pink powder made from grinding up the dried flesh of a dragonfruit. You could use dried blueberry, mango, matcha, cacao or açai powder instead, which can usually be found in health food stores. Just bear in mind that changing the powder will inevitably change the flavour and colour of the whole recipe accordingly.

SHOYU SAUCE this is another word for soy sauce in Hawai'i, and stems from the Japanese word pronounced 'shoryu'. However, this should not be confused with our house shoyu-based sauce, which is a mixture of 2 parts soy sauce, 1 part sesame oil and a splash of mirin, if you want to make your own.

TARO ROOT this is a staple in Hawaiian cooking used to make poi, lau'laus and kūlolo. It is from the kalo plant and is a bit like a white yam. Make sure you wear gloves when preparing raw taro and don't eat it raw as it can be an irritant. You could use cassava instead, or maybe sweet potato, although both would result in a slightly different taste, especially if making something like poi or kulolo.

TI LEAF this is a long, waxy, non-edible leaf used to help retain moisture while cooking. You could use banana or pandan leaves instead, both of which would flavour the food in a slightly different way. Alternatively, you can just use foil to help keep the juices in.

TOBIKO is flying fish roe, but you could use a different sort of roe if you can't get your hands on tobiko, ideally something fairly large as the eggs are about 5 mm/¼ inch across.

TOGARASHI POWDER is a zesty Japanese chilli/chili pepper spice. You could use a mix of 4 parts red chilli/chili pepper powder, 1 part sesame seeds, 1 part ground dried citrus zest and 1 part ground nori instead.

YUZU is a fragrant, sour Japanese citrus fruit, a cross between a mandarin and a lemon. The fresh fruit is hard to source but you can buy the juice from Asian supermarkets. If you can't get yuzu juice, you could use half fresh orange juice and half lime juice, although it wouldn't be quite the same.

POKE

POKE (PO-KEH)/POƱ KEI/VERB –
HAWAIIAN TO 'SLICE' OR 'DICE'.

INTRODUCING THE ISLAND POKÉ WAY.

THE CLASSIC 'AHI POKE

Here is the granddaddy of all the poke recipes. It is our standard 'ahi poke recipe and what we serve day in, day out at Island Poké. The secret to its success is the sashimi-grade 'ahi that we allow to stand on its own, without being overwhelmed with too many other flavours. If you cannot source sashimi-grade 'ahi, ask your fishmonger to advise you on whether their freshest tuna can be eaten raw.

SERVES 4 AS A MAIN

250 g/1½ cups sushi rice (see page 15)
500 g/1 lb. 2 oz. sashimi-grade 'ahi or
   yellowfin tuna (see page 15)
2 tablespoons shoyu
1 teaspoon sesame oil
3 spring onions/scallions, finely sliced
1 thumb-sized piece of fresh ginger,
   grated

OPTIONAL TOPPINGS
2 tablespoons Pickled Ginger
   (see page 139)
2 red chillies/chiles, sliced
2 spring onions/scallions, sliced
1 avocado, peeled, stoned and sliced
1 tablespoon edamame
2 tablespoons tobiko (fish roe)
2 tablespoons wakame seaweed
1 tablespoon macadamia nuts
2 tablespoons Crispy Shallots
   (see page 137)
Pineapple-Red Chilli Salsa
   (see page 134)
dash of sriracha sauce
mixed sesame seeds, for sprinkling
edible flowers, to garnish

Make up a batch of sushi rice.

Cube or dice 'ahi or tuna into smallish pieces. Place in a bowl with the shoyu, sesame oil, spring onions/scallions and ginger and gently mix together. Leave for at least 15 minutes for the flavours to combine.

Place the rice in a poke serving bowl, add the poke and garnish with any of the toppings. Add one of the following sauces: sriracha mayo (see below), wasabi crema (see below), or straight sriracha sauce.

SRIRACHA MAYO
Mix together 2 tablespoons sriracha sauce, 3 tablespoons mayonnaise, 2 tablespoons thick yogurt and the freshly squeezed juice of 1 lime.

WASABI CREMA
Stir together 125 g/½ cup sour cream, 3 tablespoons crème fraîche, 2 teaspoons wasabi paste, 1 teaspoon light soy sauce and the freshly squeezed juice of 1 lemon. Leave for at least an hour to allow the flavours to develop.

SPICY 'AHI VARIATION
Heat up a cast iron pan and char 2 jalapeños and 2 red chillies/chiles until just blistered on all sides. Remove from the pan and set aside. In the same pan, toast 1 tablespoon coriander seeds, then run a knife across them before crushing in a mortar. De-stem and finely dice the charred chillies/chiles.

Make up a Standard 'Ahi Tuna Poke (see above) and combine with above ingredients. Add a drizzle of SB Red Salsa (see page 135) if you want an extra bit of heat.

LA THREE-WAY POKE

Poke with three different soy-marinated fish – usually salmon, tuna and mahi mahi – is perfect for a big get-together. If making this recipe for 12, follow the quantities in the three fish recipes. Reduce quantities in proportion if serving fewer.

SERVES 12
If making this recipe for 12, follow Poke recipe quantities. Reduce quantities in proportion if serving fewer.

Classic 'Ahi Poke (see page 12)
Yuzu Lomi Lomi Salmon Poke (see page 18)
Mahi Mahi Poke (see below)

TO SERVE
750 g/3¾ cups sushi rice (see page 15), made with green tea or matcha
chopped chillies/chiles
Kalua Chipotle Ketchup (see page 136)
Pineapple-Red Chilli Salsa (see page 134)
Tomatillo Salsa (see page 132)

MAHI MAHI POKE
500 g/1 lb. 2 oz. very fresh mahi mahi (see page 15)
freshly squeezed juice of 2 limes
2 tablespoons shoyu
3 spring onions/scallions, finely sliced
1 thumb-sized piece of fresh ginger, grated
2 tablespoons edamame
2 tablespoons seaweed
2 tablespoons tobiko (fish roe)
1 box salad cress, snipped

SERVES 4, OR MAKES ONE-THIRD OF LA THREE-WAY POKE

Make up some green tea or matcha sushi rice. Prepare the 'Ahi Tuna and Yuzu Salmon, plus the Mahi Mahi as below.
Carefully place each poke over the rice, add some extra chillies/chiles on top. Add some extra punch with salsas and sauces, such as Kalua Chipotle Ketchup, Pineapple-Red Chilli Salsa and Tomatillo Salsa.
Eat with chopsticks, with matcha tea to sip on the side.

MAHI MAHI POKE
If you cannot guarantee the freshness of the mahi mahi, marinate the fish in the lime juice to 'cook' it for about 30 minutes. If you cannot source mahi mahi, try a similar firm fish, such as sea trout, halibut or shark.
Dice the fish and place in a serving bowl, then add the shoyu, spring onions/scallions, ginger and edamame. Sprinkle over the seaweed and tobiko. Finish with a flourish of cress.

**ENOUGH FOR 4 SERVINGS
IN POKE RECIPES**

250 g/1½ cups sushi rice
1 teaspoon salt
2 tablespoons white sugar
3 tablespoons rice vinegar
2 tablespoons mirin

BASIC SUSHI RICE

Rinse the rice at least three times in cold water. Place in a medium-sized pan with 500 ml/2 cups water and bring to the boil. After the water reaches boiling point, reduce the heat to a low simmer and cover with a lid. The rice should absorb all the water and be tender after 20 minutes.

Meanwhile, combine the salt, sugar, rice vinegar and mirin in a bowl.

Tip the rice out of the pan onto a metal tray and spread out so that it cools quickly. You can aid the cooling process by fanning. While fanning the rice, gently pour over the vinegar mixture and combine by running through the rice with a fork. Cover with clingfilm/plastic wrap if not using immediately (the cooked rice should be used within a day).

A NOTE ABOUT FISH

'AHI
Also known as yellowfin tuna.

MAHI MAHI
Also known as dorado. Use swordfish if you cannot find mahi mahi.

If using raw fish in your poke dishes, it is very important that you buy the freshest of fish, ensuring that it is sashimi-quality and can be eaten raw (check this with your fishmonger). Raw fish should always be stored in the refrigerator and eaten within 24 hours of purchase.

To check the freshness of a fish and its suitability for eating raw, there are a few guidelines:
• The eyes should be clear and plump.
• The body should be firm, plump, hydrated and shiny.
• The gills should be bright red or pink.

• Sniff the fish – if it smells unpleasant, you won't want to eat it raw.
• If buying a piece already cut from a large fish (such as tuna or salmon), the flesh should be bright in colour and hydrated.

Government food safety agencies have issued guidelines for using raw fish, as occasionally raw fish may contain parasitic larvae. If wild fish are to be eaten raw or lightly cooked, ensure that all parts of the fish, especially the thickest parts, have been frozen for at least 4 days in a domestic freezer at -15°C or colder to ensure that any undetected larvae are killed.

Before freezing, it is best to cut the fish into a block, then wrap in clingfilm/plastic wrap. To defrost, move the frozen fish to the fridge for 5–12 hours before use. Eat on the day of defrosting.

YUZU LOMI LOMI SALMON POKE

When I started street-food trading I only sold two pokes – 'Ahi Tuna and Salmon. I bought the best salmon at Billingsgate, but created this citrus-based sauce that really sets this poke apart. Use a combination of orange and lime, if you can't source yuzu.

SERVES 4

250 g/1½ cups sushi rice (see page 15)
1 teaspoon yuzu
2 tablespoons mirin
2 tablespoons light soy sauce
500 g/1 lb. 2 oz. very fresh salmon
  (see page 15)
3 spring onions/scallions
Yuzu-Mango Salsa (see page 132),
  to serve

OPTIONAL TOPPINGS

2 tablespoons edamame
1 teaspoon furikake seasoning
1 tablespoon shredded seaweed
1 teaspoon black sesame seeds
2 tablespoons Pickled Ginger
  (see page 139)
edible flowers, to garnish

Prepare a batch of sushi rice.

Make up the marinade by mixing up the yuzu, mirin and light soy. Cube the salmon and put into a bowl with enough marinade to just provide a glistening surface for the salmon. Add some very finely sliced spring onions/scallions.

Make the poke by spooning some rice into bowls, add some of the salmon, then finish by topping with the edamame beans, furikake, seaweed, black sesame seeds and pickled ginger.

To serve, add some Yuzu-Mango Salsa directly on top.

GOLDEN BEETROOT POKE

Poke, in its nature, is a fairly organic concept. It is also about championing the best ingredients. I had the idea in my early poke days to bring ingredients other than fish into my range. Golden beetroot/beets as a poke main ingredient was practically presented to me on a plate by an organic grower in Somerset who was extolling the virtues of his crop. When roasted, the golden beetroot/beet is sweet and earthy. Combined with a simple marinade, this vegetable-based poke is real crowd-pleaser.

SERVES 4

250 g/1½ cups sushi rice (see page 15)
500 g/1 lb. 2 oz. golden beetroot/
 beets or 4 medium-sized beetroot/
 beets
olive oil
salt

FOR THE MARINADE
2 teaspoons mirin
6 tablespoons soy sauce
3 tablespoons sesame oil
freshly squeezed juice of 1–2 limes
1 red chilli/chile, sliced
3 spring onions/scallions, sliced
1 thumb-sized piece of fresh ginger,
 grated

TO SERVE
2 teaspoons mixed sesame seeds
2 tablespoons Pickled Ginger
 (see page 139)
2 tablespoons edamame
1 avocado, peeled, stoned and sliced
2 tablespoons tobiko (fish roe)
 (or substitute yuzu masago for
 vegetarians)
1 tablespoon macadamia nuts, rolled
 in togarashi
1 tablespoon thinly sliced nori seaweed
edible flowers, to garnish

Prepare a batch of sushi rice.

Preheat the oven to 200°C (400°F) Gas 6.

Roll the beetroot/beets in olive oil and salt, then place in a roasting dish. Roast in the preheated oven for about 1½ hours until soft in the centre. You are really looking for the beetroot/beets to get these nice golden knobbly bits. Let them cool down, then skin the beetroot/beets and dice them up into cubes of about 1 cm/½ inch.

Prepare the marinade. Mix together the mirin, soy sauce and sesame oil. Add the lime juice, sliced chilli/chile, spring onions/scallions and grated ginger. Add the diced beetroot/beets to the marinade and leave for at least 30 minutes for the flavours to infuse.

Make up the poke by putting the rice in bowls, layer over the beetroot/beets mixture and sprinkle over the mixed sesame seeds. Add the pickled ginger, edamame, sliced avocado and tobiko (or yuzu masago for a vegetarian option). Scatter over the macadamia nuts and nori seaweed.

TIP
The beetroot/beets are easier to peel when they are still warm.

If you want to wow your friends, add some edible flowers to the finished dish.

WHAT IS POKE?

Originally, poke in the Hawaiian language was simply a term for slicing or dicing, but it came to represent a fisherman's simple meal of reef fish mixed together with crushed kukui nuts, seaweed and salt. Even though there is definitive evidence of the existence of poke predating the voyages of Captain Cook (who died in Hawai'i in 1779), some would argue the term really only took on any meaning in the 1960s.

The eventual arrival of other cultures and the availability of deep sea fish, such as 'ahi (or yellowfin tuna), changed poke, along with the particular Japanese culinary influences of including shoyu, sesame oil, tako (or octopus) and tofu in its preparation, and tsukemono (or Japanese pickles) to provide flavour balance. The poke we see on the islands today combines all these various ingredients along with some others from a diverse range of places, such as Portugal, Mexico and other Pacific regions. Poke is still considered the favourite snack in Hawai'i, being the choice for casual get-togethers, lū'aus, and eating from the back of your pick-up truck.

London, where I am now based, has suddenly become 'poke aware'! Showing up originally in the street food scene in very unlikely places, such as Fenchurch Street Station, in a Street Feast alley, and in the middle of Selfridges, it is now appearing on the menus of 'proper' restaurants in the heart of the City, in Soho, and in Canary Wharf, and is continuing to spread far and wide. What is causing this ever-expanding spread of 'pokeness'?

Perhaps it can be explained by looking at where it originally started in Hawai'i. Here poke has been seen as essentially local, casual and very much part of the food culture. It is so casual that avid poke enthusiasts insist on only buying it from a counter at their local supermarket or corner shop. It still remains fundamentally a dish made of 'ahi, tako, prawns/shrimp or tofu, with 'ahi being the top seller. The supermarket favoured is Foodland, and their poke comes piled high in big stainless steel containers. Typically ordered with two scoops of rice, and served in styrofoam trays with a bottle of sriracha sauce at hand, poke here is a no-frills experience. What makes it attractive to observers of Island cuisine is the context and the regular locals, or sometimes surfers, who munch away at their poke at the beach, in their pick-up trucks, or sitting at a bus stop.

Along comes a self-proclaimed 'Poke Godfather' from the Big Island who writes books on the subject, and takes it to Seattle of all places. His maxim, 'mo Poke, mo betta', pretty much sums up his interpretation of the dish. The community in Seattle he is targeting through his food trucks and drive-in restaurant is the expatriate Islanders, from across the Pacific. These folk want their poke super casual, with filling portions and definitely with two scoops of rice, so not really too different from what they originally could get at Foodland back in Oahu.

Step into this scenario some guys in LA who said, 'yeah, this poke looks healthy if you cut down a bit on the carbs.' They also added some flavours, some colour, plenty of sauces, and served it in trendy grab-n-go shops, targeting lean, health conscious, on-trend west siders. These shops, with nicely designed furniture, neon signs, backlit menus and ultra-smart marble and glass serving counters, were a far cry from the original basic places in Venice and Ocean Park. Success quickly followed this new presentation, alongside the new taste, and has been seen, duplicated and even surpassed by others in far-distant places from LA, such as Sydney, New York, Barcelona, Singapore, and of course London.

Here in London, at Island Poké we have actually tried to go back to the original Hawaiian form. The Aloha spirit, quality and simplicity of ingredients, the laidback approach and the transparency in sourcing are what's behind our 'island style'.

It should be added here that other near-poke dishes from around the world have been caught up in this movement. For example, E'ia Ota or Poisson Cru from Tahiti is one that has been likened to poke with its use of coconut milk and shredded coconut, ceviche from Peru by way of Mexico has been used for the lime juice marination and the extensive use of the avocado, while tataki from Japan is routinely styled into a poke for the 'pounded' ginger coatings and even searing the beef or 'ahi.

What has developed could be considered by purists back home in Hawai'i as something too far from the original. However, most poke enthusiasts would disagree and suggest that poke is merely evolving at a fast rate, just like it did on the islands from that chopped-up reef fish with a sprinkling of nuts and seaweed. The only constant is the need to keep it as close as possible to 'island style'.

SMOKED ALBACORE POKE

This poke is a great way to combine subtle flavours to enhance the smoked fish. The secret is the quality of the fish. Try cold smoking the albacore yourself, or buy from a quality supplier. This recipe is from my street-trading days, when I had a sideline in smoked fish.

SERVES 4

500 g/1 lb. 2 oz. albacore tuna
(see page 15)

FOR BRINING
2 tablespoons sea salt
3 tablespoons white sugar

TO SERVE
250 g/1½ cups jasmine rice
1½ teaspoons matcha tea, for cooking
the rice
1 small coconut, or 200 g/2 cups
freshly grated coconut
2 spring onions/scallions, sliced
150 g/5½ oz. red radishes, sliced
seaweed, to sprinkle
furikake seasoning
Chipotle Crema (see page 137)
your choice of SB Red, Tomatillo
or Yuzu-Mango Salsas
(see pages 132–135)

If you are going to smoke the fish yourself, I would suggest doing a larger amount than just enough for this recipe to make the effort worthwhile.

Prepare the fish by filleting or opening out. Start off by dry brining the fish in a mixture of salt and sugar to just cover both sides of the fish. Cover in clingfilm/plastic wrap and leave in the fridge at least overnight, but for no more than 24 hours.

When ready to smoke, remove the fish from the brine and lightly rinse in fresh water. Dry the fish on a wire rack, skin side down, for at least 1 hour.

Prepare your smoker according to the manufacturer's instructions and by getting some sawdust (I like to use applewood or oak), and start smoking. Put the fish on a rack or suspend it over the smoke for at least 12 hours at a temperature less than 35°C (95°F), replenishing the sawdust as needed. There is no need to turn the fish if it is placed on a rack.

Check to make sure the fish has formed a dry, firm, almost leathery surface and is nicely bronzed from the smoke. If you are satisfied with the result, remove from the smoker and rest on a wire rack.

Cook the jasmine rice according to the packet instructions, adding the matcha tea to the cooking water.

Prepare the fresh coconut by cracking it open, reserving the water if possible, and grating the coconut flesh.

To assemble, stir the grated coconut into the rice, moisten with the coconut water and place in bowls. Flake the smoked albacore over the rice, then add the spring onions/scallions and radishes. Finish with a sprinkle of seaweed and furikake. Spoon some Chipotle Crema on top. Serve with any combination of SB Red, Tomatillo or Yuzu-Mango salsas.

The smoked fish can be kept for up to 10 days in the fridge, wrapped in clingfilm/plastic wrap, or for up to a year if frozen.

TAKO POKE

Alongside 'Ahi Poke, Tako Poke stands as the Hawaiian favourite. Something magical happens when the tako (octopus) is combined with the marinade and poke ingredients. The transformation is remarkable, and far greater than you would expect. Although there are many variations of this recipe, this one has all the hallmarks of Hawaiian authenticity, combined with a zingy, fresh vibe. I like to serve it with my Tomatillo Salsa or additional chillies/chiles to really grab those tastebuds.

SERVES 4

500 g/1 lb. 2 oz. octopus
1 tablespoon vinegar, if cooking the
    octopus yourself
250 g/1½ cups sushi rice (see page 15)
2 tablespoons shoyu
1 teaspoon sesame oil
2 spring onions/scallions, finely sliced
150 g/5½ oz. red radishes, finely
    sliced
1 small red onion, finely diced
Tomatillo Salsa, to serve
    (see page 132)

FOR THE MARINADE
freshly squeezed juice of 1 lime
1 thumb-sized piece of fresh ginger,
    grated
4 garlic cloves, chopped

TOPPINGS
seaweed
tobiko (fish roe)
furikake seasoning
edamame
Pickled Ginger (see page 139)

If using uncooked octopus, gently simmer it whole in a pan of water with the vinegar for 1 hour, then remove from the pan and leave the octopus to cool.

Mix the marinade ingredients together in a bowl. Slice the octopus into bite-sized chunks, trying to use as much as you can. Stir into the marinade and marinate for at least 1 hour.

Prepare your sushi rice.

When ready to serve, add the shoyu and sesame oil to the octopus and mix in the spring onions/scallions, radishes and red onion.

Assemble the poke by putting the rice in bowls, followed by the octopus mixture. Top with your choice of toppings. Serve with the Tomatillo Salsa.

BEEF TRI-TIP POKE

On any Sunday in Santa Barbara you'll see a haze of barbecue smoke. Usually tri-tip beef is used – unique to the SB area, this cut is from the bottom sirloin. Here I have taken the essential tri-tip, smoky flavour and all, and made a very special poke.

SERVES 6

1.5 kg/3 lb. 5 oz. beef tri-tip, or topside corner cut or bavette/goose skirt

FOR THE DRY RUB
1 tablespoon cumin seeds
1 tablespoon coriander seeds
1 teaspoon smoked paprika
1½ tablespoons salt

FOR THE PINTO BEANS
3 slices/rashers smoked streaky bacon, chopped
150 g/5½ oz. smoked cooked ham, diced
400-g/14-oz. can chopped tomatoes
3 garlic cloves, chopped
2 teaspoons dark soy sauce
2 teaspoons ketjap manis
1 teaspoon chipotle paste
1 teaspoon smoked paprika
400-g/14-oz. can pinto beans (or black beans), drained and rinsed

TO SERVE
250 g/9 oz. kale, finely chopped
Pico de Gallo (see page 134)
SB Red Salsa (see page 135) or Kalua Chipotle Ketchup (see page 136)

If you cannot get tri-tip for you, there are two good alternatives, depending on your cooking method: use topside (preferably the corner cut) or bavette/goose skirt.

For the dry rub, heat a dry frying pan/skillet and lightly toast the cumin and coriander seeds. When slightly coloured, grind to a coarse powder using a pestle and mortar. Add the smoked paprika and salt. Rub the mixture all over the meat.

To barbecue, cook low and slow over coals or wood using the indirect method – light the coals or wood in the centre of the barbecue; when hot, move them to one side and place the meat on the other side of the rack. When cooking, use a lid with adjustable vents and top up the coals or wood as necessary. Allow at least 2 hours for a tri-tip or topside. Aim to get a nice crust and a tender medium-rare middle. If cooking bavette/goose skirt on a barbecue, cook over direct heat for about 15 minutes, turn over and cook on the other side for another 10 minutes. It should be rare in the middle.

To oven roast tri-tip or topside, start off in an oven preheated to 220°C (425°F) Gas 7 for 15 minutes to seal the surfaces, then loosely cover with foil and reduce the heat to 180°C (350°F) Gas 4 for 30 minutes or until the inside is medium-rare. Baste occasionally. Remove the foil and turn the heat up at the end of the cooking time to brown.

To cook bavette/goose skirt in a ridged pan, lightly oil the meat. Heat the pan to very hot, add the meat, leave for 3 minutes, then turn over for 3 minutes. Turn again but at right angles for another 3 minutes, then turn again at right angles for a final 3 minutes. This should give you a rare to medium-rare result. Leave a little longer if undercooked.

Make up the pinto beans. Heat up a large frying pan/skillet and add the bacon and diced ham. When browned, add the remaining ingredients apart from the beans. Turn down the heat and simmer for 20 minutes. Add the beans and 500 ml/2 cups water, and simmer for another 20 minutes.

Dice the meat into 1-cm/½-inch cubes. Place some kale in bowls, followed by the pinto beans and beef. Top with Pico de Gallo. Serve with SB Red Salsa or Kalua Chipotle Ketchup.

STICKY AUBERGINE POKE
WITH SOUR CARROT SALAD

After a stint working with a great Japanese chef in his restaurant, a number of inspirations came to mind, including this poke take on a Japanese favourite, Nasu Denganku. There are many crossovers between Hawaiian and Japanese cooking styles and culture. Although this recipe and its ingredients are less Hawaiian than Japanese, the unexpected result justifies itself and pays homage to the fusion of Japanese and Hawaiian cooking.

SERVES 4 AS AN APPETIZER

250 g/1½ cups sushi rice (see page 15)
900 g/2 lb. aubergines/eggplants
4 shallots
125 g/⅔ cup demerara/turbinado
   sugar
2 garlic cloves, crushed
1½ teaspoons crushed green
   peppercorns
75 ml/5 tablespoons soy sauce
small handful of kale, chopped
small handful of coriander/cilantro,
   chopped

FOR THE SOUR CARROT SALAD

3 spring onions/scallions
200 g/1½ cups finely grated carrots
1 tablespoon demerara/turbinado
   sugar
¼ teaspoon salt
1 tablespoon boiling water
freshly squeezed juice of 1 large lime
1 teaspoon rice wine vinegar

First make the carrot salad. Finely slice the spring onions/scallions diagonally into long strands. Mix the grated carrots and spring onions/scallions in a bowl. Dissolve the sugar and salt in the boiling water. Stir in the lime juice and vinegar and add this dressing to the carrot and onion mix. Set aside.

Prepare the sushi rice.

Cut the aubergines/eggplants into 2.5-cm/1-inch cubes. Finely slice the shallots. Have them both at hand when you are making the caramel as you will have to act quickly.

Place the sugar in a large wok set over a high heat. Swirl the wok to help melt the sugar. The sugar will have a lovely amber tone. After about 5 minutes it will start to caramelize at the edges and you will notice a caramel smell. Swirl the wok once more to distribute the caramel evenly, then add the aubergines/eggplants and shallots. Toss until the chunks are well coated, then cook for 2 minutes. Lower the heat, add the garlic and green peppercorns and cook for 2 minutes. Add the soy sauce and simmer, loosely covered with foil, for 7 minutes or until the sauce reduces to a thick consistency.

To serve, divide the carrot salad, aubergine/eggplant mixture, kale and rice between four bowls. Scatter over the coriander/cilantro.

TIP
To make this more Japanese, add a teaspoon of white miso paste before you add the soy sauce.

AGUA CHILLI SHRIMP POKE BURRITOS

One of my favourite restaurants in Southern California features this dish during their happy hour. Ideal alongside a Margarita, and my absolute favourite combo, this Mexican version of ceviche features prawns/shrimp doused in a tart and fiery agua chilli/chile sauce. Serve the sauce and garnishes on the side and let people help themselves. To make this dish more portable for picnics or easy outdoor living, serve as burritos with a twist.

SERVES 4

250 g/1½ cups sushi rice (see page 15)
Prawn/Shrimp Poke (see page 40)
1 red onion
1 large cucumber
4 standard or burrito-sized flour
    tortillas
2 avocados, peeled, stoned and sliced
handful of fresh coriander/cilantro,
    chopped
green chillies/chiles, sliced
freshly squeezed juice of 1 lime
salt

FOR THE AGUA CHILLI/CHILE
SAUCE
freshly squeezed juice of 3 limes
freshly squeezed juice of 1 lemon
4 green chillies/chiles
½ teaspoon salt
1 red onion
handful of coriander/cilantro
approx. 175 ml/¾ cup coconut water

Prepare the sushi rice and Prawn/Shrimp Poke.

To make the sauce, put the lime and lemon juices, chillies/chiles, salt, red onion and coriander/cilantro in a food processor and whizz until just puréed. Tip into a bowl and add roughly the same quantity of coconut water. Mix, adding a little more salt if necessary.

Slice the red onion into very thin rings, spread out on a plate and sprinkle a little salt over. Set aside for 10 minutes, then pat off the excess water using paper towels.

Peel the cucumber and scrape out the seeds. Cut the flesh into 1-cm/½-inch cubes and place in a separate bowl.

To serve, place a tortilla on a plate and layer up the centre with sushi rice and Prawn/Shrimp Poke, cover in Agua Chilli/Chile Sauce, add some sliced onion, cucumber, avocado, coriander/cilantro, green chillies/chiles and a dash of lime juice.

Fold the tortilla burrito-style – fold the sides inwards, then fold the top and bottom over the sides. Wrap in foil, and serve standing up or on the go. Repeat to make three more burritos.

TIP
If you want to omit the rice, substitute with some chopped Romaine lettuce.

SB-STYLE POKE

When I lived in Santa Barbara, the source of all poke was our favourite supermarket. We would buy a couple of the offerings and corn chips, and eat it on the beach after riding some waves in the morning. Looking back on it, this was beach culture at its finest. The casual combination of any really fresh fish you have on hand makes this poke super easy. If the quality of your fish is not suitable to be eaten completely raw, simply make it up in a light ceviche marinade. Try serving this poke with corn chips or in warmed corn tortillas.

SERVES 4

500 g/1 lb. 2 oz. very fresh white fish
   (such as halibut), and/or raw
   prawns/shrimp, peeled, and/or
   lobster (see page 15)
2 teaspoons yuzu
2 tablespoons shoyu
freshly squeezed juice of 1 lemon
freshly squeezed juice of 1 lime

TO SERVE
furikake seasoning
handful of Crispy Shallots
   (see page 137)
1 red onion, finely sliced
2 jalapeños, finely diced
handful of coriander/cilantro,
   chopped
corn tortilla chips, or mini corn
   tortillas

Prepare the fish by dicing it into bite-sized chunks. If using lobster, just use the tail and claw meat.

If you wish to serve the fish and/or seafood raw, simply toss it in a light dressing of yuzu, shoyu and a drizzle of lemon juice. To prepare ceviche-style, marinate in equal quantities of lemon and lime juice for 30 minutes. When ready to serve, discard the marinade to avoid 'over-cooking' the fish.

Serve the fish and/or seafood garnished with some or all of the following: furikake, Crispy Shallots, finely sliced red onion, finely diced jalapeños, and chopped coriander/cilantro.

Serve with corn tortilla chips, or over warmed mini corn tortillas.

POKE NACHOS

Our Broadgate store is in the heart of London, surrounded by city people, particularly bankers, meaning our colourful Hawaiian style makes a striking contradiction to its grey surroundings. This dish is one of the most popular items on the menu here. Nachos are generally an extremely casual dish to dip into while having some beers. Poke nachos, on the other hand, lift the dish to another level, making the ordinary nacho, well, ordinary. Great for a casual get-together with friends, and if you're looking for a great partnership, serve with Hawaiian beer from The Kona Brewing Company. My favourite is 'The Big Wave'.

SERVES 3 AS A SNACK
Choose one or more pokes of your choice:

'Ahi Poke (see page 12)
Prawn/Shrimp Poke (see page 40)
Yuzu Lomi Lomi Salmon Poke
   (see page 18)
corn chips

TO SERVE
Pico de Gallo (see page 134)
Tomatillo Salsa (see page 132)
Red Chilli Salsa (see page 133)
sliced jalapeños and radish cress,
   to garnish (optional)

Make up a portion of your favourite poke, such as 'Ahi Poke, Prawn/Shrimp Poke or Yuzu Lomi Lomi Salmon Poke.
   Make up the salsas – you should serve at least two.
   Place the poke in the middle of a large serving plate and surround with the corn chips. Serve the salsas in separate bowls with the garnishes, if you like.

POKE INARI CUPS
OR SEATTLE POKE CUPS

This is a great recipe I've adapted from some Japanese-American street food folks in Seattle. The essential thing here is a Japanese slant on the poke itself, served in their wraps, and garnished with Japanese favourites. Ideal for parties as a canapé, I would suggest going the whole way and doing a variety of three pokes to provide a range of flavours in your cups.

SERVES 4

12 inari pouches (also called inari pockets or wraps)
250 g/1½ cups sushi rice (see page 15)
200 g/7 oz. 'Ahi Poke (see page 12)
200 g/7 oz. Prawn/Shrimp Poke (see below)
200 g/7 oz. Smoked Albacore Poke (see page 27)

FOR THE PRAWN/SHRIMP POKE
500 g/1 lb. 2 oz. very fresh raw prawns/shrimp, peeled
freshly squeezed juice of 1 lime
2 teaspoons yuzu
2 tablespoons coriander seeds
1 red onion, very thinly sliced
2 tablespoons shoyu
1 teaspoon chia seeds
1 teaspoon crumbed nori seaweed

TO SERVE
2 tablespoons tobiko (fish roe)
2 tablespoons nori seaweed
3 tablespoons bean curd
3 spring onions/scallions, finely sliced
sriracha
3 small chillies/chiles, finely diced

To make the prawn/shrimp poke, place the raw peeled prawns/shrimp in a bowl with the lime juice and yuzu. Marinate for 30–60 minutes.

Toast the coriander seeds in a dry frying pan/skillet, stirring to ensure they do not burn, then grind using a pestle and mortar. Add to the marinade with the red onion for the final 15 minutes of marinating. When ready to serve, add the shoyu, chia seeds and nori seaweed.

Take an inari pouch and shape into a top-loadable cup. Put a little sushi rice in the bottom, fill with a choice of up to three different fish pokes. Add tobiko, nori and a small amount of bean curd, and top with spring onions/scallions. Repeat to make 11 more cups. Pour a little poke marinade into each cup to moisten.

Typically serve individually as canapés or as a plate of three different pockets. Have sriracha, finely diced chillies/chiles and more marinade on the side for seasoning to taste.

TIP
The quantities given here for the prawn/shrimp poke will feed four as a regular poke bowl. If using with other poke fillings for the inari pouches, you can halve the quantities.

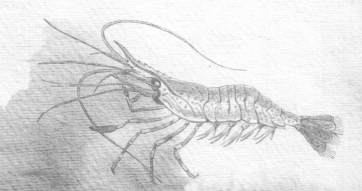

POKE TACOS

Here's where Hawaiian poke meets Southern Californian style, resulting in something quite special. The secret ingredient that makes all the difference is the soft corn tortilla. It is worth the extra effort of making your own as you go, using masa harina. If you prefer, there are a number of places to buy them ready-made. These are best served with a couple of salsas, the all-important sliced avocado and some freshly sliced jalapeños.

SERVES 4
Choose one or more pokes of your choice:

'Ahi Poke (see page 12)
Prawn/Shrimp Poke (see page 40)
Yuzu Lomi Lomi Salmon Poke
(see page 18)

8 regular-sized corn tortillas
(or better still, make your own
– see below)
2 avocados, peeled and stoned
freshly squeezed juice of 1 lime
handful of coriander/cilantro
2 jalapeños

FOR HOME-MADE TORTILLAS
75 g/⅔ cup masa harina
pinch of salt

TO SERVE
Pico de Gallo (see page 134)
Tomatillo Salsa (see page 132)
Red Chilli Salsa (see page 133)

Make up a poke of your choice, or make up two, or even three if you're having a real get-together.

Make up two or three salsas of your choice.

Prep your garnishes by slicing the avocados and drizzling with a little lime juice, chopping the coriander/cilantro, and thinly slicing the jalapeños.

If making your own tortillas, mix the masa harina and salt in a bowl with 50 ml/3½ tablespoons water to make a smooth, dryish dough. If it's too dry, add a sprinkle of water; if it's too wet, add more masa harina. Put the dough in the fridge to rest for 15 minutes. Divide the dough into eight (for 15-cm/6-inch tortillas) or twelve balls (for 10-cm/4-inch tortillas), and rest for a further 15 minutes.

Flatten a dough ball in a tortilla press (or place between two pieces of clingfilm/plastic wrap and flatten with a rolling pin to a thickness of 3 mm/⅛ inch). Heat up a dry cast iron frying pan/skillet over a high heat. Add the tortilla and cook – a few minutes on each side should be sufficient, as the surface should be slightly blistered, not carbonized. Repeat with the remaining dough balls and stack in a warmer (such as a dry, cast iron pan), ready for use.

Now get everything on the table, tortillas in their warmer in the middle, and let everyone assemble their own tacos as they please.

TIP
Smaller tortillas are more flexible if you want people to try a few different tacos, larger ones are better if serving one or two per person.

LOCAL ISLAND
FAVOURITES

CULT DISHES LOVED BY THE LOCALS.

PIPIKAULA

The name Pipikaula literally translates as 'beef rope' in Hawaiian. Sitting alongside the different trays of poke in the deli counters, you will usually find this Hawaiian-style beef jerky. It should be more moist and tender than the usual tough, leathery biltong-style jerky. Typically this dish would be taken to a luau or to the beach and shared around, eaten as a pupu (or snack) rather than as a main course.

MAKES APPROX 1.5 KG/3 LB. 5 OZ.

1.8 kg/4 lb. flank steak
sesame seeds and spring onions/
  scallions, finely sliced, to garnish

FOR THE MARINADE
235 ml/1 cup soy sauce
120 ml/½ cup sake or dry sherry
2 tablespoons liquid smoke
2 tablespoons brown cane sugar
  (or use brown or demerara/
  turbinado)
2 teaspoons sea salt flakes
¼ teaspoon freshly ground black
  pepper
1 tablespoon finely chopped fresh
  ginger
2 garlic cloves, finely chopped
2 red chillies/chiles, deseeded
  and finely chopped

Pound the beef with a mallet or wooden spoon to tenderize. Cutting along the grain, slice the steak into strips approx. 4 cm/1½ inches wide.

Combine the marinade ingredients in a large mixing bowl. Add the meat to the mixing bowl and coat fully in the marinade. Cover and refrigerate for 24 hours, turning the steak slices occasionally to ensure the marinade is well absorbed.

Drain the meat. Discard the marinade.

Place a cooling rack on top of a baking sheet covered in baking parchment. Arrange the meat pieces so they lay flat on the cooling rack.

Dry the meat in the oven at around 80°C (175°F) for 7–8 hours, until the beef gets a 'jerky' texture. If you have a dehydrator or dry box, you can use this instead, although it will take a bit longer (at least two days in a hot sun with the box being brought in at night).

To serve, cut slices diagonally (about 1 cm/½ inch thick) and garnish with sesame seeds and spring onions/scallions. Eat with chopsticks, sharing with friends and enjoying 'pupu' style.

TIP

For a more tropical twist, try swapping the soy sauce for 235 ml/1 cup pineapple juice.

The dried meat may be stored in an airtight container in the refrigerator for up to 5 days, or in the freezer, wrapped, for 6–8 months.

LEMON CAPER MAHI MAHI

Mahi mahi (also known by its Spanish name, dorado) is probably the second most popular fish in Hawai'i, after 'ahi. Mahi mahi is firm and meaty, like a white version of tuna, and is similar in texture to swordfish. I'm not sure of the history of this particular dish, but it graces the menus of reputable establishments across the islands, from popular food trucks to high-end hotel restaurants. I should think it's derived from the Italian dish piccata, a traditional Milanese offering of sautéed veal with a lemon, butter and caper sauce, which was favoured by the southern Italians as a great way to serve their fresh catches of fish. Whatever its origins, this is a deliciously satisfying dish guaranteed to please your tastebuds and impress your guests!

SERVES 2

2 mahi mahi fillets (swordfish or
   sea bass work nicely too)
60 g/½ cup plain/all-purpose flour
3 tablespoons olive oil
45 g/3 tablespoons butter
4 tablespoons freshly squeezed
   lemon juice
2 tablespoons capers, drained
2 tablespoons chopped garlic
lemon slices and radish cress,
   to garnish (optional)
Hawaiian sea salt
freshly ground black pepper

Cut the fish fillets into smaller portions, approx. 5 x 7.5 cm/ 2 x 3 inches in size. Tip the flour onto a plate and evenly coat the fish on all sides.

Heat the oil in a frying pan/skillet over a medium heat. Add the butter and melt down until it starts to foam. Add the fish and sauté for approx. 5 minutes on each side or until lightly browned and golden.

Transfer the cooked fish to a plate lined with paper towels to absorb any excess oil. Leave any remaining butter/ oil in the pan. Season the fish with salt and pepper and keep warm.

Combine the lemon juice, capers and garlic in a small bowl. Pour the mixture into the frying pan/skillet with the leftover butter/oil. Gently simmer over a low heat until the garlic is cooked through.

Serve the fish immediately on a bed of rice, salad or Ulu Mash (see page 128) and top with the lemon caper sauce. Garnish with lemon slices and radish cress, if you like.

TIP
This sauce also works well with chicken or prawns/shrimp, served on a base of pasta, such as linguine.

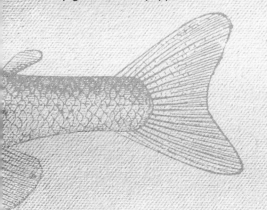

'AHI KATSU

As with many popular dishes in Hawai'i, this one has Japanese roots and has become a real staple in the islands. This version of 'ahi Katsu is slightly fancier than the original local favourite, with an added layer of nori seaweed to give that extra umami element, but the recipe can just as easily be made without the nori and with pork, chicken, squid or another fish (such as mahi mahi/dorado or even cod or halibut) instead of the 'ahi.

SERVES 12

900 g/2 lb. 'ahi or yellowfin tuna
  fillets
1 tablespoon salt
1 tablespoon freshly ground black
  pepper
130 g/1 cup plain/all-purpose flour
4 eggs
100 g/2 cups panko breadcrumbs
8 sheets of nori seaweed
vegetable oil, for frying

FOR THE SAUCE
100 ml/⅓ cup light shoyu sauce
2 tablespoons dry mustard, mixed
  with a little water to make a paste
225 g/1 cup mayonnaise

TO SERVE
steamed white rice
furikake seasoning

Cut the fish into slices roughly 18 cm/7 inches long and 2.5 cm/1 inch thick.

You will need three wide, shallow bowls. In the first bowl, mix the salt, pepper and flour. Break the eggs into the second bowl and beat them with a fork. Put all the panko breadcrumbs into the third bowl.

Wrap each fillet of fish in a sheet of nori so the seaweed overlaps. Lightly wet the tip of your finger in water and run it along the edge of the nori to help it stick and stay wrapped around the 'ahi. Dip each fillet into the flour mixture, then in the egg wash and finally coat with the panko breadcrumbs.

Shallow-fry the breadcrumbed fillets in vegetable oil over a medium heat, for 2–3 minutes on each side, turning frequently until evenly browned and golden. Place on a plate covered in paper towels to drain away the excess oil, then slice.

For the sauce, mix together the shoyu, mustard paste and mayonnaise and serve as a side sauce, along with some steamed white rice and furikake.

ISLAND LIFE

Hawai'i is a magical place, there's no doubt about it. The islands are volcanic and the impressive 'mauna' (or mountains) dominate the landscape. Each island is its own little microcosm, with the south and west being typically hotter, drier and more arid and the north and east sides being breezier, rainier and more lush. Having said that, wherever you are on any of the islands, you are never far from both the mountains and the ocean. Whichever side of the island you're on, it will be cooler, greyer and wetter the closer you are to the mountains.

Because the islands are surrounded by the impressive and vast Pacific Ocean, native Hawaiians were, and still are, heavily influenced by the waters around them. Fish and octopus have always been staples in the Hawaiian diet. However, islanders appreciate the need to nurture both the land and sea in order to sustain a healthy, balanced environment. Fishing ponds were set up all over the islands, a protected space in shallow waters sheltered by a manmade lava rock wall where small fish could safely grow. This ensured the fish stocks were kept plentiful, allowing the locals to take what they needed, when they needed it.

There are many different fishing techniques used by Hawaiians. 'Throwing net' is one of the more traditional methods, whereby a fisherman carefully stalks the coastline until he sees a school of fish, then casts his net out into the air so that it lands on top of the fish, enabling him to scoop up the net with his fresh catch inside. A team effort is known as a 'hukilau' where entire communities, including the 'keiki' (or children), come together to help pull in a large net set out near the shoreline. The catch is shared out between all the different families.

Fish hooks were traditionally carved from bone, shell or sometimes wood. The fishing line and nets were made from a native Hawaiian plant called 'olonā', a relative of the stinging nettle. Apart from fishing from the shoreline, nets and lines were used to fish from the 'wa'a' (or canoes) out in deeper waters. In more recent years I've seen lines or nets

*Left to right:
Nāpali Coast State
Wilderness Park,
northwest of Kauai
Island; Palm trees
on the Big Island of
Hawai'i; Ala Moana
Beach Park, located
between Waikiki and
Honolulu; A surfer
rides a wave, Hawai'i,
1963; Surfboard
decoration in a
garden on Huelo
Island, north of Maui.*

thrown out from all sorts of floating vessels, including kayaks and stand-up paddleboards. 'Spearfishing', 'surrounding' and 'laying net' continue to be used locally as means to source fish.

Fishing, in its many forms, as well as other water-based activities, particularly Hawai'i's best known pastime, surfing, play a large role in the day-to-day life of native islanders. Mornings often start off with a Spam Musubi (see page 71), Kona coffee and a quick trip to the nearest beach or lookout point to check the water, affectionately known as a 'surf check' or 'dawn patrol'. Depending on the tides, swells, waves, winds and weather in general, they will make a call on what the day's initial activities will be. If the waves are good, locals head to the beach to surf or to watch the surfers gliding through the waves. If the water is flat, they might consider paddleboarding or diving. If there's a full moon and lots of jellyfish, they might opt for a waterfall hike instead!

Most Hawaiians are early risers. Apart from when they party – and they definitely enjoy a good 'pā'ina' – most islanders go to sleep fairly early and rise at the crack of dawn, if not before. They are in tune with the natural cycles of nature around them and there is no doubt that 'Mama Honua' (or Mother Nature) is the boss. Hawaiians have a healthy respect for their surroundings and are humble enough to appreciate that in an instant they could be taken out by a tsunami, hurricane or volcano, so as a race of people they very much 'live in the moment' and cherish their beautiful islands. I've noticed that when I ask people how they are over there, the response is usually 'I'm great' or 'fantastic' or 'amazing'... starkly contrasted by the 'alright's and 'okay's I usually get when asking the same question in London. That continues to be one of the things that really warms me about Island Poké – seeing the genuinely positive effect our food has on people's moods. It's such an honour to be able to share the gift of Aloha and put a smile on someone's face with something as simple as a poke bowl!

SESAME GINGER FISH

An easy recipe where the sauce is the star of the show. The toasted sesame mixed with the sweetness of the honey and the saltiness of the shoyu is one of those really moreish combinations. Make extra to mix with mayonnaise for an island style version of tartare sauce. It also works nicely with things like chicken, aubergine/eggplant or prawns/shrimp.

SERVES 4

450 g/1 lb. fish fillets, such as salmon
   or halibut, deboned
vegetable oil, for greasing
1 bunch spring onions/scallions, finely
   sliced, to garnish (green bits only)
1 teaspoon toasted sesame seeds,
   to garnish

FOR THE SAUCE

1 tablespoon finely chopped fresh
   ginger
1 tablespoon sesame seeds
2 tablespoons honey
2 tablespoons shoyu
freshly ground black pepper

TO SERVE

Pickled Ginger (see page 139)
steamed green vegetables
steamed white rice

Mix together all the sauce ingredients in a small bowl. Brush generously over the fish.

Brush a grill/broiler pan, non-stick griddle pan or barbecue with vegetable oil.

Grill or sear the fish fillets over a medium-high heat for a few minutes on each side, depending on the type of fish, size of the fillets and how well you like your fish cooked.

Garnish with spring onions/scallions and the toasted sesame seeds. Serve immediately with Pickled Ginger, steamed green veg and the Hawaiian starch of choice – steamed white rice.

TŪTŪ'S SOMEN SALAD

'Tūtū' means 'Grandma' in Hawaiian and Somen is a thin (or the thinnest) type of Japanese wheat noodle. This casual, easy dish is simple to throw together and serve at a barbecue or as part of a luau-style feast. In true island style, this recipe is relaxed and flexible with plenty of room to add your own personal touch by swapping out or adding in some extra chopped, cooked meats or vegetables.

SERVES 6 AS AN APPETIZER OR SIDE DISH

250-g/9-oz. pack somen noodles
1 lettuce, shredded
1 carrot, grated
1–2 cucumbers, deseeded and julienned
200 g/7 oz. kamaboko (Japanese fish cake), slivered
200 g/7 oz. cooked ham, shredded
1 egg, beaten, fried and cut into 1-cm/½-inch strips
furikake seasoning

FOR THE SAUCE
120 ml/½ cup soy sauce
120 ml/½ cup chicken stock
100 g/½ cup sugar
60 ml/¼ cup rice vinegar
2 tablespoons sesame oil

Boil the somen noodles as instructed on the packet, rinse in cold water, drain and put onto a platter. Chill.

In a saucepan, combine all the sauce ingredients. Bring to the boil, lower the heat and simmer for 5 minutes. Set aside to cool.

Layer the lettuce, grated carrots and cucumbers over the noodles. Top with the sliced kamaboko, ham and egg. Chill before serving.

Pour the sauce over the salad just before serving and sprinkle with furikake.

Great with pickles – try any combination of Pickled Ginger, Cucumber Pickles and Pickled Scotch Bonnets (see page 139).

TIP
Replace the ham with salami, cooked chicken or bacon, or flaked, smoked fish. If you want a bit more veg, you can also try adding steamed and chopped broccoli, asparagus or green beans, or even a can of sweetcorn/corn.

Kamaboko can be purchased in oriental supermarkets, but you can replace it with imitation crab if you wish.

AUNTY'S FISH PATTIES

In Hawai'i everyone is one big family, so pretty much any female who is older than you is referred to as 'Aunty'. The first time I tried these little patties was when my friend's mum made them, hence the name. She used a local Hawaiian fish known as Ō'io. In the absence of Ō'io, I would suggest using something like halibut or sole.

MAKES 8 PATTIES

3 eggs, lightly beaten
1 teaspoon salt
60 g/½ cup plain/all-purpose flour
2 teaspoons baking powder
400 g/14 oz. fish fillets (such as halibut or sole), finely chopped
6 spring onions/scallions, finely sliced
4 peeled water chestnuts, chopped
vegetable oil, for frying

Pour the lightly beaten eggs into a large mixing bowl and add in the salt, flour and baking powder. Mix in the fish, spring onions/scallions and water chestnuts.

Heat some vegetable oil in a large, heavy-based frying pan/skillet over a medium-high heat. When the oil is hot, use a large serving spoon to pour the mixture into the pan in individual patties. These should look almost like little omelettes, approx. 7 cm/2¾ inches in diameter. Fry for a few minutes or until brown, before flipping over and cooking on the other side.

Serve with steamed white rice and spinach/collard greens.

TIP
You can substitute the raw fish meat with pretty much any cooked, flaked fish, or even a smoked fish. You can also swap out the water chestnuts for another crunchy vegetable, such as asparagus, green beans or sweetcorn/corn. Also, coconut oil is good for frying the patties.

SHOYU CHICKEN

This is almost every Hawaiian's favourite dish and is so easy to make. Like all popular recipes, there are many versions, but this method, courtesy of Lauren's uncle, has stuck because the ingredients are things I generally have in my kitchen. The salty savouriness of the soy sauce with the chicken makes this a warm, comforting dish. Traditionally, locals use chicken thighs with the skin on and bone in, but I prefer using boneless, skinless chicken thighs and adding some skinless chicken breast too.

SERVES 6

450 g/1 lb. boneless, skinless
    chicken breasts
450 g/1 lb. boneless, skinless
    chicken thighs
235 ml/1 cup soy sauce
200 g/1 cup brown sugar
1 tablespoon apple cider vinegar
1 tablespoon Worcestershire sauce
1 heaped tablespoon finely chopped
    fresh ginger
1 heaped tablespoon finely chopped
    garlic
sticky white rice, to serve
Cucumber Pickles (see page 139),
    sliced spring onions/scallions, or
    sesame seeds, to garnish (optional)

Combine all the ingredients, apart from the garnishes, in a storage container or ziplock bag with 235 ml/1 cup water. Marinate overnight in the refrigerator or for a minimum of 8 hours.

Tip the ingredients into a large, heavy-based stew pot and bring to the boil over a high heat, stirring occasionally to ensure nothing sticks to the bottom of the pot. Once boiling, reduce the heat to low, cover and simmer for 30 minutes or until the chicken is tender and cooked through. Stir occasionally and skim the fat off the top as necessary.

Using a slotted spoon, remove the chicken from the pot and place on a chopping board or serving platter. Loosely cover with foil to keep warm.

Bring the sauce back to the boil, reduce the heat and simmer for 10 minutes. Remove from the heat and let the sauce cool for 10 minutes, allowing it to thicken slightly.

Serve with sticky white rice and drizzle the remaining sauce over the rice and chicken. Garnish with Cucumber Pickles, sliced spring onions/scallions or sesame seeds.

TIP
For a thicker gravy, add 3 tablespoons cornflour/cornstarch mixed with a little water after you remove the chicken from the pot. Or, after removing the chicken from the pot and while the sauce is reducing, shred the chicken meat, then add it back into the reduced sauce. Serve immediately.

Great with some pickles on the side and our take on Hawaiian chilli pepper water, SB Red Salsa (see page 135).

DRUNKEN OCTOPUS PŪPŪS

The word 'pūpū' in Hawaiian generally refers to a bite-sized snack, like an hors d'oeuvre. Pūpūs are often served at gatherings on platters and include savoury island treats, such as poke, smoked tako, calamari or sashimi. The concept of a pūpū platter has been adopted by mainland America as a sort of pan-Asian selection of canapés. These days it can include anything from chicken wings or nachos to dim sum, sushi or crudités and dips.

SERVES 6 AS AN APPETIZER

1 octopus
1 can of beer
2 tablespoons shoyu
1 tablespoon sesame oil
2 teaspoons cornflour/cornstarch
1 tablespoon sugar
sliced spring onions/scallions or
   toasted sesame seeds, to garnish

Either beat the octopus 500 times with a wooden mallet and a handful of Hawaiian sea salt or freeze it for a month until it gets tender.

Boil the tenderized octopus in a large pan of water for approx. 30 minutes, depending on the size. After about 20 minutes, test the octopus by prodding it with a wooden spoon. The meat should be just firm but still soft and tender. Do not overboil as it will become tough and rubbery. Once cooked, drain the octopus.

Scrape off the black outside layer of skin with a spoon or the back end of a knife (or feel free to use your hands, island style!). Slice the skinned meat into bite-sized pieces.

Pour two-thirds of the beer into a frying pan/skillet (drink the remaining third yourself!). Add the octopus and fry for just a couple of minutes. Once most of the beer in the pan has been absorbed by the octopus, add the shoyu and sesame oil.

Mix the cornflour/cornstarch with a little water to form a liquid paste and add to the pan. Once the cornflour/cornstarch is blended in, add the sugar and heat for another few minutes.

Serve in a shallow bowl, garnished with sliced spring onions/scallions or toasted sesame seeds. Eat with either toothpicks/cocktail sticks or chopsticks.

If you wish, serve some salsas as dipping sauces, including Burnt Corn Salsa (see page 132), Pineapple- Red Chilli Salsa (see page 134) and SB Red Salsa (see page 135).

UNKO'S SALMON SCRAPS
WITH GUAVA PONZU

A Fish Fry is your standard post-fishing activity in Hawai'i, where everyone comes together while the daily catch is fried in batches and served as it comes, along with a selection of dipping sauces, for all to enjoy. This particular recipe is for a fish fry with a fruity ponzu, but it is easily adaptable to personal preference and depending on fish/fruit availability.

MAKES 120 ML/½ CUP DIPPING SAUCE

any firm fish fillets, for frying (salmon belly works well) – as much as you want to fry
mochiko rice flour (or cornflour/ cornstarch), for dusting
vegetable oil, for frying

FOR THE GUAVA PONZU SAUCE
4 tablespoons light soy sauce
3 tablespoons white vinegar
freshly squeezed juice of ½ lemon
1 teaspoon vegetable oil
3½ tablespoons tangy fruit juice of your choice, such as guava, yuzu or pineapple
crushed black pepper

To make the guava ponzu, mix the soy sauce, vinegar, lemon juice, oil and pepper together in a bowl. Squeeze in the guava juice (or a similar amount of juice from the fruit of your choice – I also like pineapple). Set aside.

Roll the fish fillets in the mochiko flour (or cornflour/ cornstarch). The moisture from the fish should be enough to make the flour stick.

Heat some vegetable oil in a frying pan/skillet until hot, ensuring the base of the pan is generously covered in oil so the fish doesn't stick and burn. Fry the fish for a minute or two on each side, depending on the size of the fillets. You may need to cook the fish in batches, to avoid overcrowding the pan.

Remove the fish using a slotted spatula and set on a plate lined with paper towels to drain the oil.

Serve immediately on a bed of white rice with some steamed greens, the Guava Ponzu dipping sauce and a wedge of lime.

LOCO MOCO

Loco Moco is about as local as it gets. Originating on the Big Island of Hawai'i not long after the Second World War, Loco Moco can now be found at almost every local café, diner or lunch truck across the Islands. It is a mountain of comfort food, stacking a hamburger patty and fried egg on top of rice and covering the whole thing in a thick beef and onion gravy. This dish can be eaten at any time of the day, but I love it as a relaxed island style Sunday brunch.

SERVES 4

FOR THE GRAVY
vegetable oil, for frying
1 onion, sliced
125 g/4½ oz. mushrooms, sliced
2 teaspoons soy sauce
500 ml/2 cups beef stock
1 tablespoon cornflour/cornstarch
salt and freshly ground black pepper, to taste

FOR THE BURGERS
500 g/1 lb. 2 oz. minced/ground beef
1½ tablespoons soy sauce
2 teaspoons Worcestershire sauce
½ teaspoon freshly ground black pepper
2 garlic cloves, finely chopped
vegetable oil, for frying

TO SERVE
500 g/2½ cups Calrose rice (medium grain rice), steamed
4 eggs, fried
spring onions/scallions, finely sliced, to garnish

To start the gravy, heat a little oil in a large frying pan/skillet over a medium heat. Add the onion and fry for a few minutes until brown. Reduce the heat to medium-low and caramelize the onions for 10–15 minutes. Remove the onions from the pan and set aside.

To make the burgers, combine all the burger ingredients (except the oil) in a bowl and mix well, then form into four equally-sized patties, approx. 10 cm/4 inches in diameter. Using the same frying pan/skillet, heat a little oil and cook the burgers for approx. 4 minutes on each side, or until browned. Remove from the pan and set aside.

Still using the same pan, add the mushrooms and sauté over a medium heat until browned. Season with a little salt and pepper. Add the caramelized onions back into the pan and stir in the soy sauce and beef stock. Bring to a simmer.

Mix the cornflour/cornstarch with 1 tablespoon water to make a liquid paste, then stir into the pan and simmer for a further minute or two, until thickened. Season with a little more salt and pepper, to taste.

To serve, put a quarter of the rice on each plate. Top with a burger (sliced or left whole, depending on your preference) and smother in the onion and mushroom gravy. Top off with a fried egg and garnish with finely sliced spring onions/scallions and cracked black pepper.

TIP
Try this with Pickled Shiitakes (see page 140)and Kalua Chipotle Ketchup (see page 136).

SPAM MUSUBI

Hawai'i is the world's largest consumer of Spam. With many still viewing this as a wartime meat option, it sounds unappealing but is surprisingly lovable. When caramelized in a teriyaki-style sauce, Spam has a sweet, salty, smoky flavour which is balanced perfectly by the sticky white rice. Variations include replacing Spam with Shoyu Chicken (see page 63) or Unko's Salmon Scraps (see page 67), or adding an egg layer between the Spam and the rice.

SERVES 6

200-g/7-oz. can Spam
3 tablespoons soy sauce
2 tablespoons mirin
2 tablespoons sugar
300 g/3 cups cooked Calrose
   (medium grain) or Japanese rice
1 tablespoon furikake seasoning
2 sheets of nori, each sheet cut into
   3 strips 5 cm/2 inches wide
vegetable oil, for frying

Slice the Spam into six slices, approx 5 mm/¼ inch thick.

Heat some oil in a non-stick frying pan/skillet and fry the Spam slices for 1–1½ minutes on each side until nicely browned and a bit crispy. Transfer the Spam slices to a plate and drain the pan.

Reduce the heat and add the soy sauce, mirin and sugar to the pan. Mix well. Return the Spam slices to the pan and coat well in the sauce, simmering for 1–1½ minutes so the sauce thickens and caramelizes. Remove from the heat.

To create the musubi, shape the cooked rice into six little pillows, approx. 8 x 5 cm/3¼ x 2 inches and roughly 4 cm/1½ inches high. Sprinkle a little furikake on top of each rice pillow and top with a slice of Spam.

Place a strip of nori seaweed, shiny side down, on a clean, dry surface. Lay a musubi across the centre of the nori and fold the nori strip around the width of the musubi so it wraps around the Spam and rice, holding them both together. Using a little water on the tip of your finger, dampen the end of the nori strip and stick it down. Repeat with the rest.

Serve immediately or wrap in clingfilm/plastic wrap and take out with you as a snack.

TIP
If you wish, place a fried egg or scrambled egg omelette on top of the Spam before wrapping in the nori. Or replace the Spam with salmon from Unko's Salmon Scraps (see page 67) or with chicken from Shoyu Chicken (see page 63) and top with sliced avocado before wrapping in the nori.

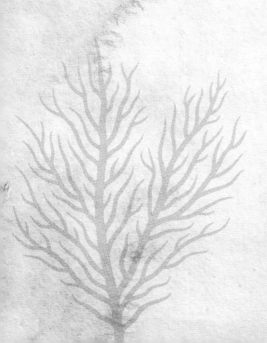

HURRICANE POPCORN

A firm favourite with Hawaiians, this popcorn is fantastic on its own as a tasty snack. For the real thing, try using the best natural popcorn you can find and avoid the ones that are packaged with butter substitutes.

SERVES 4

2 tablespoons furikake seasoning
2 tablespoons sesame seeds
1 tablespoon vegetable oil
150 g/5½ oz. chicken skin, e.g. the skin from 2 leg joints
½ teaspoon Maldon sea salt
100 g/7 tablespoons salted butter
1 tablespoon coconut oil
150 g/¾ cup good-quality natural or plain popcorn kernels (definitely not the microwave-in-a-bag variety)

Grind the furikake and sesame seeds using a pestle and mortar. Set aside.

Heat the vegetable oil in a pan and add the chicken skin. Gently fry until golden and crispy, then drain on paper towels. Put into a food processor and whizz up with the salt to a breadcrumb consistency. Scrape out and set aside.

Melt the butter in a small pan. Set aside.

Heat up the coconut oil in a large, heavy-based lidded pan until fairly hot. Put a few kernels of popcorn in the pan. When they pop, add the rest and spread out in the oil. Put the lid on and leave the pan undisturbed for at least 30 seconds. When you hear the corn starting to pop, start shaking the pan to avoid it burning (lift it off the heat if necessary). Before fully popped, carefully lift the lid to let steam out, to avoid moisture forming on the popcorn.

Mix the melted butter into the popcorn, add the furikake mixture and mix all with the chicken skin. Serve.

TIP
For an authentic local touch, mix in 100 g/3½ oz. Mochi Crunch (Japanese arare rice crackers) to the popcorn.

PACIFIC RIM
FUSION

DISHES THAT SHAPE THE PACIFIC'S
CULINARY IDENTITY.

POISSON CRU

Poisson Cru is Tahiti's answer to poke or ceviche, made using freshly squeezed coconut milk and lime juice. Literally meaning 'raw fish' in French, it is typically made using tuna which has been well rinsed in salt water to remove any traces of blood, but you can also use a fresh, meaty white fish instead, such as swordfish or mahi mahi (also known as dorado).

SERVES 4

900 g/2 lb. very fresh firm fish fillets, cut into 2 x 5-cm/¾ x 2-inch pieces

1 tablespoon rock salt

1 green (bell) pepper, deseeded and cut into 2 x 5-cm/¾ x 2-inch pieces

1 large cucumber, deseeded and roughly peeled so that some skin is left on

2 x 400-ml/14-fl oz. cans coconut milk

1 large carrot, half cut into 2 x 5-cm/¾ x 2-inch pieces and half cut into matchsticks

freshly squeezed juice of 7 limes (approx 120 ml/½ cup lime juice)

5 medium tomatoes, cut into 2 x 5-cm/¾ x 2-inch pieces

1 spring onion/scallion, finely sliced, to garnish (optional)

Rinse the fish in running water or soak it in salted water for about 5 minutes, then drain and place in a large glass or stainless steel mixing bowl.

Sprinkle the rock salt over the fish pieces and mix. Add the (bell) pepper, cucumber and coconut milk. Gently mix together with your hands to avoid breaking up the fish. Add the carrot pieces (not the matchsticks) and lime juice; gently mix again. Add the tomatoes and gently mix again.

Wipe the rim of the bowl down and cover with clingfilm/plastic wrap. Marinate in the fridge for a minimum of 2 hours to allow the flavours to infuse.

Before serving, add the carrot matchsticks and sliced spring onion/scallion as a garnish.

TIP

Try frying some corn tortillas in a little coconut oil until golden, then top with a large heaped spoonful of Poisson Cru and serve with guacamole and a wedge of lime.

If taking to a party or displaying in front of guests, you can line a serving dish with layers of lettuce (Romaine lettuce works well) as a base and then add the Poisson Cru. Top with the carrot matchsticks and some grated lime zest and eat as little lettuce wrap parcels.

Great served with Tomatillo Salsa (see page 132) on the side.

FURIKAKE CALAMARI

This is an easy, but really fun and tasty dish to whip up. I tend to use only squid rings, but you can also use the tentacles if you wish. Make sure you buy squid that is fresh and has already been cleaned. I pre-soak my squid before cooking to make sure it's tender, and the panko and sesame from the furikake add a satisfyingly crunchy element to this local favourite.

**SERVES 4 AS AN APPETIZER
OR 2 AS A MAIN COURSE**

225 g/8 oz. squid tubes, sliced
  into rings
buttermilk, coconut milk or salt
  water, for soaking
4 egg whites
120 ml/½ cup milk
60 g/½ cup plain/all-purpose flour
100 g/2 cups panko breadcrumbs
40 g/¼ cup polenta/cornmeal
1 very small shallot, very finely diced
2 tablespoons cane sugar
3 tablespoons furikake seasoning
rapeseed/canola oil, for frying
Sriracha Mayo (see page 12), to serve

Soak the squid in buttermilk, coconut milk or salt water for approx. 30 minutes, then rinse clean with water and dry using paper towels.

Mix the egg whites and milk together in a shallow dish.

Combine the flour, panko breadcrumbs, polenta/cornmeal, shallot, sugar and furikake in a separate shallow dish.

Lay three sheets of paper towels on a plate and set aside.

Thoroughly coat the squid rings in the egg mixture, opening the rings to ensure an even coating. Next, thoroughly coat the squid in the breadcrumb mixture, again ensuring the insides of the rings are well coated.

Pour enough oil into a wok to a depth of about 5 cm/2 inches and heat over a high heat.

Fry approx. 10 squid rings at a time in the wok, turning once. When both sides are brown, transfer to the paper-lined plate, then fry the rest in batches. Serve with Sriracha Mayo for dipping.

TIP
This dish can also be made using 'ahi, mahi mahi or bite-sized boneless, skinless chicken pieces instead of the squid. If serving as a main course, serve alongside some other pokes such as Sticky Aubergine Poke (see page 32).

SEA BASS CRUDO

This is about as far from Hawai'i as you can get, yet still feel the connection with the raw fish. I've spent quite a bit of time in Italy, mostly Florence, but also in Puglia in the south. The fish, clams and shellfish served in Puglia are very fresh and simply prepared — crudo accurately defines how they like things. This is a great dish for gatherings, a sharing starter, or on its own with an Aperol Spritz.

SERVES 4

4 very fresh sea bass fillets
freshly squeezed juice of 1 lemon
freshly squeezed juice of 1 lime
150 g/5½ oz. red radishes
150 g/5½ oz. daikon radish
1 small red onion
handful of flat-leaf parsley
olive oil
1 tablespoon red peppercorns,
   crushed
salt

Thinly slice the sea bass and place neatly on a serving plate. Drizzle with half the lemon and lime juices and add a sprinkle of salt.

Very thinly slice the radishes, daikon and red onion. Roughly chop the parsley. Combine these together and mix with the remaining citrus juices, and add a little olive oil.

Scatter over the fish, add a little more olive oil, and the crushed red peppercorns, and serve.

EATING IN HAWAI'I TODAY

There are two ways of looking at what is happening today with eating in Hawai'i. One is to study the great island chefs and their restaurant menus, the other is to look at what Hawaiians cook and eat on an everyday basis.

Although the 50th State adheres in most part to mainland food trends, there is a distinct Asian-Pacific character that is reflected in the style of cooking known as Hawaiian Regional Cuisine. This was initiated in the 1990s by a group of 12 island chefs. The aim was to bring together local suppliers, including farmers, ranchers, fishermen and those working in hospitality to increase the awareness of indigenous produce and recipes. This had the effect of reducing the mainland-based menus and the dependence on shipped-in ingredients – notably Spam would remain untouched by this movement.

Hawaiian Regional cooking is not a unique island-based style, but a fusion style drawn from the many cultural influences in Hawai'i. Today, many menus on the islands feature a number of dishes in this style, sometimes sitting incongruously alongside Napoli-style pizza, smashed burgers and venison chops. Importantly, there is a distinction now in providing ingredient provenance that proudly announces local sources. Rather than putting too much effort into creating new fusion recipes, chefs are producing more familiar dishes with carefully sourced local ingredients. Examples of this include Kamehameha burgers made with Big Island Dustin Ranch beef, salad greens from Waipoli, Maui onions, and vine-ripened tomatoes from Hau'ula.

In the last decade, Regional Cooking, alongside local sourcing, has had a profound affect on the consumer's approach to buying ingredients for cooking at home, and where they choose to dine.

The continuing pleasure and popularity in Hawai'i of having an old-school plate lunch could be a metaphor for the central Hawaiian need for heartiness and comfort food above all else. Dishes such as kalua pork, shoyu chicken and loco moco are expected to be served in generous portions.

Unusually for a non-islander, 7-Eleven is one of the most popular destinations for a takeout. Although not a gourmet destination, islanders go there for food that is comforting, microwaveable, quick and easy. Some say that food trends in Hawai'i can be judged by the products 7-Eleven are adding and deleting from the lines in their stores. It is plainly apparent that apart from the Slurpee machine, Spam

Left to right: Handmade banners on a farm in Kauai; An old shack with local fruits and coconut drinks for sale in Waiahole, Oahu, Hawai'i; A taro field in Hanalei, Hawai'i; A bowl of miso ramen.

musubi is a perennial favourite with at least ten varieties on sale. There are also the expected local must-haves, including fried simian, manapua, teriyaki burger, kim chee fried rice and tonkatsu pork ramen. Interesting new offerings on the shelves include bento boxes, beef pho and shu mai dumplings, described as shrimp pork hash (note the folksy title of this dish instead of the non-fusion original).

The consistent appeal in Hawai'i of certain variations of imported dishes that defies all the fusion, health and local source trends, is a result of the conservative islander approach of keeping things simple and very much as they were. These dishes include such things as 'baked spaghetti', corned beef hash, Portuguese sausage, biscuits and gravy, SoCal-style tacos and doughnuts and waffles.

In contrast to these favourites, island dishes that are considered 'native' still hold their own with Spam musubi, poke and ramen being exceptionally trendy. The ever-increasing popularity of poke can be appreciated right from the neighbourhood Foodland supermarket to the best island restaurants. The local Foodland minimart offerings are considered some of the best and are presented in copious quantities on their counters. In contrast, some restaurants are

offering 'poke flights' of three different varieties in delicate portions. These pokes may include 'ahi with seaweed and kukui nuts, kim chee tako, and hamachi, using yellowtail, with accompaniments such as avocado-yuzu mousse and fish roe.

What does this mean? The Hawaiian today is bombarded by health advice, commercial interests, ecological concerns and food trends, just as on the mainland. The significant difference is the distance itself to the mainland and other Pacific Rim countries. The paradox of the remoteness combined with the closeness of today's communication is another curious reality in Hawai'i. There's very much a seasonal comfort food sense in Hawai'i matching the seasons on the mainland. In the autumn/fall, for example, menus across the island feature pumpkin pie, roast pork and apples with cinnamon – despite the fact that summer never seems to end on Hawai'i.

In a food sense, it appears islanders get by through sticking to what they know above all else. Through the initiatives of their celebrity chefs, this conservatism has now been combined with a new awareness of food provenance and creative fusion cooking. It all adds up to what is actually a real melting pot of the Pacific.

SAMOAN OKA

Poké in a South Pacific style unique to Samoa is what oka is all about. When I first tasted it, I knew I was somewhere very different from Hawai'i. The Samoans go all-out for maximum taste and quantities. There's a very big flavour contribution from the coconut, which balances the intensity of the marinade. The coconut is, in fact, what sets oka apart from what we normally imagine poke to be. This is our take on oka – it is more of a soupy consistency than Hawaiian poke and perfect served on its own as a sharing starter in small bowls, or in huge portions if you are trying to be authentically Samoan.

SERVES 6

1 fresh coconut
1 kg/2¼ lb. very fresh white fish fillets
   – you need one or two types, such
   as hake and/or pollock
freshly squeezed juice of 2 limes
freshly squeezed juice of 1 lemon
2 teaspoons shoyu
2 teaspoons mirin, plus extra to serve
1 red onion, roughly chopped
1 red chilli/chile, chopped, plus extra
   to serve
handful of coriander/cilantro,
   chopped, plus extra to serve
3 spring onions/scallions, thinly sliced
150 g/5½ oz. cherry tomatoes, thinly
   sliced
150 g/5½ oz. red radishes, thinly
   sliced
200 g/7 oz. daikon radish, thinly
   sliced
200 g/7 oz. cucumber, thinly sliced
400-ml/14-oz. can coconut milk
2 tablespoons Crispy Shallots
   (see page 137)
2 tablespoons tobiko (fish roe)

Prepare the coconut by cracking it open and reserving the coconut water. Peel and grate the coconut flesh and set aside.

Dice the fish into small cubes and place in a bowl. Drizzle half the lime and lemon juices over the fish and add the shoyu and mirin. Leave the fish to marinate for about 30 minutes.

Transfer the fish to a serving bowl. Add the red onion, chilli/chile, coriander/cilantro, spring onions/scallions, tomatoes, red radishes, daikon and cucumber. Add the coconut milk to loosen things up, along with the reserved coconut water and then add the remaining citrus juices. Scatter over and lightly stir in the grated coconut.

Drizzle over some more mirin and scatter over some extra chilli/chile and coriander/cilantro if you want that extra punch. Finish off with some Crispy Shallots and a little tobiko.

Serve alongside some pickles, including Cucumber, Scotch Bonnets and Shiitakes (see pages 138–140).

TERIYAKI BURGER

Affectionately known as 'teri burgers', these are Hawai'i's take on this American classic. The teri sauce gives these burgers a sweet, sticky quality and helps to keep the meat moist and extra succulent. Although I have suggested frying, they are arguably even better cooked on the barbecue or grilled/broiled.

MAKES 4

450 g/1 lb. minced/ground steak
1 bunch spring onions/scallions, finely sliced (white and green parts)
1 teaspoon finely chopped fresh ginger
1 teaspoon finely chopped garlic
¼ teaspoon freshly ground black pepper
¼ teaspoon sea salt
2½ tablespoons Teriyaki Sauce (see page 136)
10 g/¼ cup panko breadcrumbs
1 tablespoon toasted sesame seeds
2 tablespoons vegetable oil
4 burger buns, warmed (brioche buns work well)
thinly sliced red onion, lettuce and tomato, to serve
Kalua Chipotle Ketchup (see page 136)
Cucumber Pickles (see page 139)

Place the steak in a large bowl with the spring onions/scallions, ginger, garlic, pepper, salt, Teriyaki Sauce, panko breadcrumbs and sesame seeds. Mix together well. Divide the mixture into four burgers and shape into round patties, approx. 2.5 cm/1 inch thick.

Heat the oil in a heavy-based frying pan/skillet over a medium-high heat. Fry the burgers for approx. 4 minutes on each side, or for a little longer if you prefer your burger well-done.

Serve each burger in a warm bun with thinly sliced red onion, lettuce and tomato. Serve with Kalua Chipotle Ketchup on the side along with some Cucumber Pickles.

TIP
For an extra tropical twist, try topping each of your burgers with a grilled/broiled pineapple ring.

MISO BUTTERFISH

One of my favourite recipes. To ensure the fish is flavoursome and really melts in the mouth, marinate it for 2–3 days before cooking. This recipe is a great option for entertaining as, apart from being utterly delicious and guaranteed to impress, you can prep it in advance. Try serving it with Pickled Ginger (see page 139).

SERVES 4

4 x 200-g/7-oz. black cod fillets, or sablefish (Chilean sea bass and salmon also work well)
235 ml/1 cup sake
235 ml/1 cup mirin
250 g/1 cup white miso paste
150 g/¾ cup granulated sugar
1 tablespoon furikake seasoning
25 g/⅓ cup spring onions/scallions, finely sliced (optional)

Rinse the fish. Gently but thoroughly pat dry with paper towels. Set aside.

Place the sake and mirin in a heavy-based pan and bring to the boil over a high heat. Boil for a few minutes to cook off the alcohol, then simmer for 10 minutes.

Whisk in the miso paste until fully dissolved. Add the sugar, stirring continuously to make sure it doesn't stick to the bottom of the pan and burn. Simmer over a low heat for about 45 minutes, stirring occasionally. The marinade will thicken slightly and caramelize. Cool to room temperature.

Once the marinade has cooled completely, put three-quarters into a non-metallic, sealable storage container or ziplock bag. Add the fish, ensuring it is completely coated. Refrigerate for 2–3 days, stirring occasionally to ensure the fish is well marinated. Reserve the remaining marinade in the fridge to use later – some for cooking and some for serving.

Preheat the oven to 180°C (350°F) Gas 4.

Remove the fish from the marinade, but leave a good coating on the fish. Lay the fish on a baking sheet and bake in the preheated oven for about 10 minutes.

Preheat the grill/broiler to medium-high. Pour a little of the reserved marinade over each baked fish fillet and grill/broil for 3–5 minutes, or until golden brown and caramelized.

Drizzle any remaining marinade over the fish, sprinkle with furikake, and top with sliced spring onions/scallions. Serve immediately with steamed greens and rice.

TIP
You can also use this marinade recipe with chicken, just cook it for a little longer in the oven, ensuring the meat is cooked through before you put it under the grill/broiler.

TOSTADITOS DE MARISCOS

When you invite friends over and feel the need to cook something out of the ordinary, taking things solidly 'south of the border' could be the answer. These impressive morsels are poke dressed up as fancy Mexican antojitos. They can be served very casually, or you can dress them up and show off your culinary skills. Either way, the result is something special. The combination here truly is greater than the sum of its parts.

SERVES 6

750 g/1 lb. 10 oz. any combination of very fresh fish fillets, octopus and/or prawns/shrimp
6 corn tortillas (see page 43 for making your own)
sriracha sauce, to serve

FOR THE MARINADE
freshly squeezed juice of 2 lemons
1 red onion, finely sliced
1 tablespoon coriander seeds, toasted
1 tablespoon shoyu
1 tablespoon mirin

FOR THE SALSA
2 slightly firm avocados, peeled, stoned and diced
1 red onion, finely chopped
2 jalapeños, finely chopped
handful of coriander/cilantro, chopped
freshly squeezed juice of 1 lime
salt

Cut your choice of fish, octopus and/or prawns/shrimp into bite-sized pieces. Place in a large bowl, add the marinade ingredients and stir together. Marinate for a maximum of 30 minutes.

Mix all the salsa ingredients together in a separate bowl, adding salt to taste.

Heat up a dry cast iron pan and toast the tortillas on both sides until charred.

To serve, place the avocado salsa on the toasted tortillas, top with the marinated fish or seafood, then drizzle over sriracha sauce to taste.

BAJA FISH TACOS

Baja California can be considered the best place to find a really good fish taco. All the ingredients are there, along with the variety of salsas that bring a good fish taco together. A fish taco depends on the freshness of the fish, the quality of the tortilla and the punchiness of the salsas, contrasted against the creaminess of the crema.

SERVES 4

1 tablespoon cumin seeds

1 tablespoon coriander seeds

1 teaspoon smoked paprika

½ teaspoon salt

800 g/1¾ lb. white fish fillets, such as pollock, hake, snapper or any easy-to-fillet flat fish

flour, for dusting

2 tablespoons vegetable oil

8 small corn or flour tortillas (flour is more authentic for Baja style, but corn is my choice)

1 ripe avocado, peeled, stoned and sliced

1 lime, sliced

salt and freshly ground black pepper

FOR THE CREMA

2 tablespoons mayonnaise

4 tablespoons Greek-style yogurt

1 teaspoon SB Red Salsa (see page 135) or Tabasco sauce

FOR THE SLAW

400 g/14 oz. white cabbage, coarsely shredded

1 carrot, coarsely grated

½ onion, thinly sliced

Make up the crema by mixing together the mayonnaise, yogurt and the Salsa or Tabasco. Set aside.

Combine the cabbage, carrot and onion into a slaw. Set aside.

Heat up a small, dry frying pan/skillet and lightly toast the cumin and coriander seeds. When slightly coloured, grind to a coarse powder using a pestle and mortar. Add the smoked paprika and salt. Rub this mixture all over the fish fillets and set aside for at least 30 minutes.

Prepare the fish by slicing it into manageable portions for eight tacos, then dust in flour combined with a little salt and pepper. Heat the oil in a frying pan/skillet and fry the fish in two batches until just slightly browned and cooked through. Transfer to a plate lined with paper towels to drain, then keep warm.

Heat a cast iron pan to warm the tortillas until slightly charred and warmed through.

Make up the tacos by placing some of the slaw on each tortilla, add the fish and drizzle over the crema. Serve with slices of avocado and lime.

I suggest serving with Tomatillo Salsa, Pico de Gallo and SB Red Salsa (see pages 132–135). If you want something extra, try including some Pickled Scotch Bonnets and Cucumber Pickles (see page 139) on the side.

KIMCHI CRABCAKES

This is one of my favourite dishes to cook for a special dinner or summer lunch. The crabcakes are lovely served with a potato salad and some fresh rocket/arugula or spinach drizzled in olive oil. The light, golden panko crumbs are the perfect match for the soft, sweet crabmeat and the tanginess of both the lime and kimchi cut through the crabcakes beautifully.

SERVES 6 AS A MAIN COURSE OR 12 AS AN APPETIZER

2 limes
85 g/3 oz. kimchi, drained and finely chopped
1 large egg
115 g/½ cup mayonnaise
½ teaspoon rock salt
½ teaspoon freshly ground black pepper
85 g/2 cups panko breadcrumbs
225-g/8-oz. can crabmeat, drained
225 g/8 oz. king crab/jumbo crabmeat
4 tablespoons rapeseed/canola oil
Sriracha Mayo (see page 12), to serve
Miso Tenderstem Broccoli (see page 128), to serve

Finely zest one of the limes then cut both of the limes into six wedges so you have 12 in total. Transfer the lime zest into a large bowl and set the wedges aside.

Add the kimchi, egg, mayonnaise, salt and pepper to the bowl with the lime zest. Using a fork, mix until well combined before adding half of the panko breadcrumbs and all of the crabmeat. Put the remaining panko breadcrumbs in a shallow dish.

Divide the crabmeat mixture into 12 equal portions and shape into little crabcake patties. Transfer the cakes to the panko dish and generously coat both sides in the breadcrumbs. Place the cakes on a baking sheet lined with baking parchment, cover lightly with clingfilm/plastic wrap and refrigerate for 30 minutes.

Heat the oil in a large frying pan/skillet over a medium heat. When the oil is hot and has started simmering, it's time to cook the crabcakes. Add the crabcakes in batches, four at a time, and cook for approx. 3 minutes per side until golden. Transfer to a cooling rack set over paper towels to drain. Repeat with the remaining crabcakes.

Serve immediately with the lime wedges, home-made Sriracha Mayo and Miso Tenderstem Broccoli.

LOBSTER QUESADILLAS

When invited over to a friend's house for a little backyard feast in Santa Barbara, these quesadillas were one of my favourites. I know lobster is a luxurious ingredient that requires a bit of an event to justify it, but these will take centre stage when having a summer cook-up with your friends. We always relied on our friend JC to get the lobsters; hopefully you can come up with a similar arrangement.

SERVES 4

1 medium lobster tail
   or 8 langoustines
knob/pat of butter
a little vegetable oil
freshly squeezed juice of 1 lime
8 corn tortillas
200 g/2 cups grated Cheddar cheese,
   or similar
1 ripe avocado, peeled, stoned and
   thinly sliced
SB Red Salsa (see page 135) or
   Tabasco sauce, to drizzle
handful of coriander/cilantro leaves,
   to garnish

FOR THE CARAMELIZED ONIONS
1 red onion
knob/pat of butter
1 tablespoon demerara/turbinado
   sugar

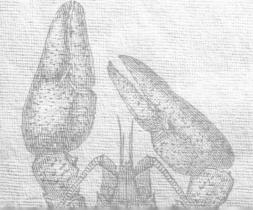

First make the caramelized onions. Slice the onion into very thin rings. Melt the knob/pat of butter in a pan, add the onion rings and slowly sauté until soft. Add the sugar and continue cooking with the lid on for approx. 15 minutes until they have a jammy consistency; if dry, add a little water.

To prepare the lobster or langoustines, use scissors to cut down the shell, making sure you don't snag the meat when you do this. Heat the knob/pat of butter and a little oil in a frying pan/skillet, add the lobster or langoustines and sauté over a medium-high heat for 3 minutes on each side until just barely cooked through (it/they will finish cooking in the heated quesadillas). Add the lime juice to deglaze the pan and set aside to cool.

Remove the meat from the shell and chop into bite-sized pieces.

Place a corn tortilla in a cast iron frying pan/skillet preheated to a medium-high temperature. Quickly place a handful of Cheddar on top and spread out. Scatter a quarter of the lobster or langoustine meat over, add a tablespoon of the caramelized onions, add a little more cheese, then top with another corn tortilla.

When the bottom tortilla is warmed through, you will be able to lift a corner and see some charring, then flip it over to the other side using a spatula and heat to the same slightly charred level. Beware of overcooking – they should be slightly charred. Repeat with the remaining tortillas and filling.

Tip the cooled lobster cooking juices over the sliced avocado and serve on the side with a drizzle of SB Red Salsa to taste and scattered with coriander/cilantro leaves.

'AHI GINGER POTSTICKERS

This is a fun way to serve your 'Ahi Shoyu Poke, cooked. Potstickers are basically Japanese gyoza and these little dumplings are the perfect combination of soft and steamed on one side while still being crispy golden-brown on the other. The salty savouriness of the shoyu with the warmth of the ginger make this dumpling filling so right you'll wonder why you've never had it before. Team up with a selection of our dipping sauces and/or condiments such as furikake seasoning.

SERVES 4

450 g/1 lb. Classic 'Ahi Poke
  (see page 12)
140-g/5-oz. can water chestnuts,
  drained
1 egg, beaten
20 gyoza wrappers
vegetable oil, for greasing

TO SERVE
Shoyu Sauce (see page 9)
Pickled Ginger (see page 139)
spring onions/scallions, sliced

Put the 'Ahi Poke into a blender or food processor with the water chestnuts and egg. Gently pulse until you have a textured, slightly chunky mousse. If the mixture seems too dry, you can add another egg.

Lay out the gyoza wrappers, 'Ahi Poke filling and a shallow bowl of water side by side.

Taking one wrapper at a time, lay it out flat and spoon 1 large tablespoon of the filling into the centre of the wrapper. Using a finger, wet the edges of the gyoza wrapper with water. Fold the wrapper in half and gently press around the edges to seal together. Repeat to make 20 potstickers.

Heat a frying pan/skillet to a medium-high heat. Once hot, use some paper towels to carefully grease the pan with a little oil – you need just enough to coat the surface.

Place the potstickers into the pan, cover with a lid and cook for 2 minutes. Lift up the lid, add 3–4 tablespoons water around the pan to create steam and quickly replace the lid. Cook the potstickers for another 3–4 minutes. Do not turn. They should be golden-brown and crispy on the bottom with a steamed dumpling texture on top.

Serve immediately with Shoyu Sauce and Pineapple Ketchup as dipping sauces, plus Pickled Ginger on the side. Garnish with sesame seeds or sliced spring onions/scallions.

TIP
Try swapping the 'Ahi Poke for another poke – the Sticky Aubergine Poke (see page 32) works particularly well.

PACIFIC CHOWDER

Unrelated to New England or Manhattan chowders, this one is based in the middle of the Pacific, combining influences from the expat communities in Hawai'i to produce a Pacific fusion. Vary the dish according to what's available at the fishmongers.

SERVES 6

1 kg/2 ¼ lb. fish, diced or sliced
250 g/2½ cups white or brown basmati rice
200 g/7 oz. yard-long beans (or any green beans)
150 g/5½ oz. okra
200 g/7 oz. spicy chorizo
200 g/7 oz. mixed celery, carrot and onion, all finely chopped
small piece of galangal, finely chopped
1 teaspoon ground turmeric
3 garlic cloves, finely chopped
1 tablespoon olive oil
400-ml/14-fl oz. can coconut milk
1 glass white wine
1 small onion, chopped
500 g/1 lb. 2 oz. any combination of fresh clams, mussels and prawns/shrimp
150 g/5½ oz. sugar snap peas
red chilli/chile, chopped, to taste
1 teaspoon nam pla sauce
2 teaspoons light soy sauce
salt

TO SERVE
freshly grated coconut, to garnish
sriracha sauce
chopped red chillies/chiles
Pineapple-Red Chilli Salsa (see page 134)

Cut the fish into boneless cubes or portions of fillets.

Cook the rice according to the packet instructions, then drain and set aside.

Steam or boil the yard-long (or other green) beans and okra until al dente. Cut into bite-sized pieces.

Chop the chorizo into small pieces and cook in a pan for about 5 minutes, until it starts to brown and release its oil. Leave to cool in the pan.

Sauté the celery, carrot and onion in a large pan with the oil from the chorizo pan. When they are beginning to become coloured but not browned, add the galangal, turmeric and garlic. When just starting to release that garlic aroma, add the olive oil and fish into the sauce. Cook over a medium heat for about 5–10 minutes (this depends on the thickness of the fish) and when the fish is starting to colour on the surface, add the coconut milk and stir.

Reheat the chorizo pan and deglaze with the white wine, then add the chopped onion and shellfish, cover with a lid and cook until the shellfish are just starting to open up.

Into the large pan of fish, add the cooked rice, the sugar snap peas, beans and okra, and tip in the chorizo, onion and shellfish. Add some red chilli/chile to taste and adjust the seasoning with a little salt. Top up with a little water if necessary – the sauce should have the consistency of double/heavy cream. Leave the pan on a low simmer while you add the nam pla sauce and soy sauce.

Grate some fresh coconut and scatter on top. Serve with sriracha sauce, additional chopped chillies/chiles and Pineapple-Red Chilli Salsa.

LŪʻAU INSPIRED
FEASTING

FOOD MADE FOR SHARING.

SMOKED 'AHI DIP

This dip is so quick and easy to make. If you can't get your hands on smoked 'ahi, you can use cooked tuna with a few drops of Liquid Smoke to give it that lovely smoky flavour.

SERVES 4 AS AN APPETIZER

400 g/14 oz. smoked 'ahi
2 tablespoons freshly squeezed lemon juice
3 tablespoons mayonnaise
dash of Worcestershire sauce
dash of Tabasco sauce, to taste
3 tablespoons freshly chopped chives,
   plus extra to garnish
1 tablespoon very finely diced shallot (optional)
pinch of Old Bay Seasoning (optional)
sea salt and freshly ground black pepper

TO SERVE
tortilla chips, crudités, lemon or lime wedges

Using your hands or a fork, flake the fish. Place all the ingredients into a bowl (or you can use a food processor). Mix until you have a smooth but textured consistency, ensuring there are no big chunks and that all the ingredients are well combined.

Garnish with extra chives and serve with tortilla chips or crudités and some lemon or lime wedges. You could also try serving with Pineapple and Cucumber Kimchi (see page 140) for a contrast.

TIP
For a more substantial snack, serve as a pâté on toast or have with some of our Cucumber Pickles (see page 139) as a sandwich filling. You can also use pretty much any smoked fish (smoked marlin or swordfish work well), adding more or less sour cream according to your preference. Jazz up with capers, diced (bell) pepper or chopped gherkin.

GUACAMAME DIP

A combination of two top ingredients from Hawai'i's nearest neighbours, Mexico and Japan. Similar to guacamole, but with added protein from the edamame beans.

SERVES 4–6 AS AN APPETIZER

1 ripe avocado
freshly squeezed juice of 2 limes
350 g/12 oz. edamame beans, shelled
   (defrosted if frozen)
1 tablespoon finely chopped red onion
2 tablespoons finely chopped tomato
handful of fresh coriander/cilantro, finely chopped
½ red chilli/chile, deseeded and chopped (optional)
¼ teaspoon each sea salt and freshly ground
   black pepper

Slice the avocado in half lengthways and remove the stone. Scoop the flesh into a bowl, mash with a fork and sprinkle with the lime juice. Put all the remaining ingredients in a food processor and blitz for a minute or two to a smooth, creamy consistency. Gently stir this mixture with the avocado. Taste and season, adding extra salt, lime juice or chilli/chile as necessary.

Cover and pop in the fridge for 20 minutes to help the dip chill and set, or serve immediately with lime wedges, and tortilla chips or crudités to dip.

TIP
Oven-roast some veg and serve in a toasted pitta, along with the Guacamame and some rocket/arugula. Garnish the dip with some chopped coriander/cilantro, edamame beans or sliced red chilli/chile.

CHICKEN LONG RICE

This is another lū'au favourite which can be found on plate lunches and in diners across the islands. The 'long rice' refers to the long, thin, rice noodles, aka vermicelli, which form the basis of this dish. It is a homely, comforting dish which is great served as an appetizer or as a side dish alongside other meats and vegetables.

SERVES 4

50 g/2 oz. long rice (i.e. vermicelli rice noodles)
450 g/1 lb. boneless, skinless chicken, diced
1 onion, finely chopped
2 celery stalks, sliced (optional)
1½ teaspoons finely chopped fresh ginger
600 ml/2½ cups chicken stock
2 spring onions/scallions, finely sliced
vegetable oil, for frying

Soak the noodles in warm water and leave in warm water until you are ready to use them. (They actually only need about 10 minutes to soften, but the locals do it this way, for simplicity's sake.)

Meanwhile, shallow fry the chicken in a small amount of vegetable oil until lightly browned. Add the onion and celery, if using, and cook for a few more minutes. Add the ginger and chicken stock. Cover and cook over a low heat for 1 hour or until tender.

Drain, then wash the noodles thoroughly under running water and cut into 5-cm/2-inch lengths. Add to the pan of chicken, bring to the boil, then simmer for 5–10 minutes, just to warm through. Garnish with the spring onions/scallions and serve.

TIP
For that home-made 'Pot Noodle' feel, try adding dried shiitake or porcini mushrooms. You can also add sweetcorn, asparagus, tenderstem broccoli or whatever else you fancy!

Bring in some salsas to pep things up, such as SB Red Salsa (see page 135), Red Chilli Salsa (see page 133) or Kalua Chipotle Ketchup (see page 136).

KALUA PIG (OVEN STYLE)

Traditionally, a whole kalua pig is served as the centrepiece of any lūʻau or paína (party), and it feeds the entire community. The flesh is rubbed with Hawaiian sea salt and slow cooked overnight in an underground 'imu' oven lined with stones and two types of leaves. The meat is kept moist from the leaves and has a rich, smoky flavour. The meat is then shredded, similar to pulled pork, and served 'plate lunch' style alongside other dishes like Chicken Long Rice (left) and Squid Luʻau (see page 119).

SERVES 10–12

1.8 kg/4 lb. pork shoulder
2 tablespoons Hawaiian rock salt
  (or sea salt)
2 tablespoons Liquid Smoke
1 banana leaf
4–6 large ti leaves

string, to tie up the meat

Score the meat on all sides by slashing diagonally and making slits 5 mm/¼ inch deep and approx. 2.5 cm/1 inch apart. Rub the Hawaiian salt into the slits, then rub well with the Liquid Smoke (reserve a little for later) on all sides.

Wrap the pork in the banana leaf and then wrap in the ti leaves, ensuring the meat is completely covered by leaves. Tie securely with a piece of string. Wrap the whole parcel in foil, making sure the juices will be completely sealed in to keep the meat tender. Leave to stand at room temperature for 45 minutes so that the smoky flavour is absorbed. Preheat the oven to 180°C (350°F) Gas 4.

Place the wrapped pork on a rack in a shallow roasting pan. Roast in the preheated oven for 3½ hours, then turn the heat up to 230°C (450°F) Gas 8 and roast for another 45 minutes.

Unwrap the pork and allow it to cool for 15 minutes, then shred the meat using your fingers or two forks. Allow to stand in the mild brine solution with a few additional drops of Liquid Smoke for 5 minutes before serving.

TIP
Use any leftover pork as an alternative filling for tacos (see page 95) or potsticker dumplings (see page 100). This is also a great way to cook your Christmas or Thanksgiving Turkey, giving it a tender, smokiness which is irresistible. Try mixing in some steamed cabbage or spinach/collard greens just before serving for that traditional island flavour.

KALUA BONE BROTH

A good bone broth should be as paleo and natural as possible. This Big Island version borrows from some of the intertwined culinary cultures that have come to the islands. In particular, the Japanese Tonkatsu and Chinese 'Long Life' broths are real influences. The secret is to follow the method closely for best results – don't skip any of the steps. When you are done after the long and slow simmering time, you will not only be extremely proud of the result but should be able to term it 'Hawaiian Penicillin'.

MAKES ABOUT 3 LITRES/3 QUARTS

3 kg/6½ lb. beef bones, preferably
   a combination of knuckle, rib
   and neck
1 chicken carcass
2 tablespoons molasses
100 ml/⅓ cup rice wine vinegar
2 tablespoons dark soy sauce
1 onion, quartered
1 bulb of garlic, sliced across in half
2 stems of lemongrass, crushed
handful of coriander/cilantro leaves
2 teaspoons coriander seeds

Put the beef and chicken bones in a large stock pot, cover with water and boil vigorously for at least 30 minutes.

Meanwhile, preheat the oven to its highest setting.

Take the bones out of the water (discard the water), spread out on baking sheets and put into the preheated hot oven. Keep them cooking away for as long as it takes to deeply brown them (probably 45–60 minutes). Don't worry too much that they could be 'overdone'.

When the bones are done to your satisfaction, put them back into the stock pot with 3 litres/3 quarts fresh water, or more to cover the bones. Thin the molasses with a little warm water and add to the stock pot, along with all the remaining ingredients. Bring the water up to a slow simmer, cover with a lid and keep it simmering away overnight, or for at least 9 hours. Skim the fat off and give it a stir occasionally. Top up with more water if necessary.

When the cooking time is up, remove the bones and strain the broth into a wide shallow tray or dish to cool rapidly. To aid the cooling, stand a large glass full of ice cubes in the tray or dish. This process should eliminate potential bacterial growth. Pour the cooled broth into suitable containers and refrigerate when completely cooled down. It will be good for at least a month in the fridge, or for years if frozen.

THE SPIRIT OF ALOHA

Aloha is not only one of the most important words in the Hawaiian language, it is a way of being, and is also an integral part of the Hawaiian culture. Family, community, respect, sharing and making a personal, positive contribution are all values Hawaiians aspire to live by, and the spirit of Aloha embodies these beliefs. However, in the last 50 years or so, the word 'Aloha' has become somewhat bastardized by the rest of the world and is now synonymous with tropical vacations, tiki bars and plastic flower leis. Despite this, the deep-rooted sentiment contained within this humble word is far grander and more sacred than simply implying a 'hello' or 'goodbye'.

There are a few ways we can interpret the literal meaning of the word, but this particular one has always resonated the most with me. In Hawaiian, the word 'Alo' can refer to a person being present in the moment, or it can refer to the way in which we outwardly present ourselves. The word 'Hā' means 'breath of life' and encompasses the belief that when we breathe correctly with focus and intent, we intensify our 'Mana' (Hawai'i's term for chi, prana or spiritual energy), therefore sharpening our connection with the outside world and increasing our own ability to create positive change.

The combination of these two words into 'Aloha' could be explained as a directive, a guide on how to live righteously, to be at one. If 'alo' is the external, the human face you present to the world and the mask you choose to wear, then 'hā' is the internal, your inherently good spirit and its power to manifest the reality you desire. By living with Aloha in our day-to-day lives, we create balance from the inside out, aligning our internal with the external in a perfectly harmonious match.

Aloha is basically the essence of unconditional love and should always come from the heart, so remember that it goes beyond being just a warm welcome, a fond farewell, an act of kindness or a friendly gesture... it truly is indicative of the spirit

*Left to right:
A woman making
a hat from palm
leaves; Flower leis
on display at a store
on Maunakea Street;
A selection of
traditional lu'au food;
oven-style Kalua
Pig; A traditional
Imu oven used to
slow-cook meat.*

of joy and giving that we are all capable of and which the Hawaiian people carry with pride.

So for us, the words 'Hawaiian inspired' go beyond just referring to the birthplace of poke. The Hawaiian people, along with their love and respect for the 'Aina' (or land) inspire us not only with their sense of Aloha, but also with their laidback and inclusive approach to cooking, eating and socializing. When Hawaiians prepare food, they make extra to share and when they catch fish or pound poi, they gift portions to friends and neighbours. They take real pride in being part of a community and sharing the Aloha, so coming together to eat in abundance is an important part of bonding within the Hawaiian culture.

A Lū'au is a celebratory feast and an opportunity for people to unite and pay respects to, or show appreciation for, a particular occasion, from a first birthday to a loved one's passing, and a whole variety of events in between. Food is plentiful, with all

guests making a contribution to a delicious banquet. No one arrives empty-handed and no one goes without a good portion.

An Imu is a traditional Hawaiian oven dug into the earth, lined with volcanic rocks and banana leaves. This is used to slow cook the meat at the feast, making it tender and juicy with a wonderfully smoky flavour and aroma. Kalua Pig (see page 109) is normally the centrepiece of the Lū'au, cooked in the imu until the meat falls off the bone.

Food is often served buffet-style on large trays for everyone to help themselves, even when eating at home. This assortment of local dishes all hold their own on the plate while uniting to showcase the tastiest produce from around the islands. The Kalua pork will typically be accompanied by other Hawaiian favourites such as Lau'Laus (see page 116), Squid Lu'au (see page 119), Classic 'Ahi Poke (see page 12), Chicken Long Rice (see page 108) and Haupia Macadamia Pie (see page 144).

LAU'LAU

Lau means leaf in Hawaiian and Lau'Laus are individual parcels of cubed meat and fish wrapped in two different types of native Hawaiian leaf, one edible and one not. Outside of Hawai'i, I suggest using the more widely available large spinach leaves or collard greens to replace the kalo (or taro) leaf as the edible inner layer of the parcel, and a banana or pandan leaf to replace the outer layer, which will help keep the meat tender. Lau'Laus are normally made in large batches and are a favourite at lū'aus or for school fundraisers. Even when given the recipe, I had to scale the ingredient quantities down from 50 portions to one!

SERVES 2

8 large collard greens/spinach leaves, washed and destalked

100 g/3½ oz. beef, cut into 2.5-cm/ 1-inch cubes

100 g/3½ oz. pork (fatty shoulder), cut into 2.5-cm/1-inch cubes

100 g/3½ oz. butterfish (or salmon), boned and cut into 2.5-cm/ 1-inch cubes

100 g/3½ oz. taro (or sweet potato/ yam), peeled and cut into 2.5-cm/ 1-inch cubes

pa'akai (or any rock salt)

2 ti leaves (or banana leaves), wiped clean and destalked

a steamer

To make each parcel, lay out two of the large collard greens/ spinach leaves so they are overlapping in a cross shape. Take half the cubes of meat, fish and taro (or sweet potato/yam) and put in the centre of the leaves. Sprinkle over a little salt on top of the cubes and wrap the leaf up tight in a little parcel. Repeat the wrapping process with two more of the same leaves on the same parcel. Use a ti or banana leaf as a final wrapping layer, pulling up the sides and tying securely.

Repeat the wrapping process with the remaining leaves and filling.

Traditionally you would slit the last ti leaf in the middle and poke the other end through, creating a little bow, but for simplicity's sake you can just wrap in foil twice, sealing tightly so all the juices and moisture stay in.

Steam the parcels for 2 hours, then serve with steamed white rice or Chicken Long Rice (see page 108).

SQUID LU'AU

This recipe is another old Hawaiian favourite, normally served as a side at a lū'au or on a 'plate lunch'. This dish is normally made with squid, but chicken has become an equally popular option. Squid lu'au looks a little like creamed spinach, but with a touch of sweetness from the coconut milk. Lu'au leaves are traditionally used for this dish but it's important to boil them in water for at least 1 hour to remove any toxins before using. Here, we have adapted the recipe for ease and used spinach instead; it doesn't need to be cooked first and is easier to source outside of Hawai'i.

SERVES 4

2 teaspoons Hawaiian salt
450 g/1 lb. squid, cleaned and sliced
large knob/pat of butter
¼ onion, finely diced
900 g/2 lb. fresh spinach/collard
  greens, washed and destalked
350 ml/scant 1½ cups coconut milk
120 ml/½ cup evaporated skimmed
  milk

Cut the squid into bite-sized pieces.

Melt the butter in a heavy-based pan and gently sauté the squid for 2–3 minutes. Add the onion and continue sautéing for another couple of minutes, or until the squid is nearly cooked through. Take care not to overcook the squid.

Add the spinach/collard greens, coconut milk and evaporated skimmed milk to the pan. Cover with a lid and gently simmer over a low heat for approx. 30 minutes until thickened and stewed. Turn off the heat and keep warm until you are ready to serve.

Serve 'plate lunch' style alongside other lu'au dishes such as Kalua Pig (see page 109) and Chicken Long Rice (see page 108).

TIP
If you don't fancy squid, just substitute it with chicken and swap out 235 ml/1 cup of coconut milk for chicken stock.

PAPAYA & AVO CRAYFISH CUPS

These are fun little appetizers if you're entertaining as they're not too heavy but are packed with flavour. Think of this almost like a lighter, island style Marie Rose dish. It is actually my mother's recipe and she is a big fan of the papaya-avo-roasted mac nut combination. Even without the crayfish and simply served as a salad, this medley of flavours is a real winner.

SERVES 4 AS AN APPETIZER

4 ripe avocados
2 ripe papayas
150 g/5½ oz. cooked crayfish, drained
1 spring onion/scallion, finely sliced
Papaya Seed Dressing (see below)
2 Little Gem/Bibb lettuces, washed
150 g/5½ oz. macadamia nut halves,
    roasted
salt and freshly ground black pepper
lime wedges, to serve

PAPAYA SEED DRESSING
6 heaped tablespoons mayonnaise
freshly squeezed juice of 1 lemon
2 tablespoons white wine vinegar
seeds from 2 papayas
    (used above)

Peel the avocados and papayas and stone and deseed. Reserve the papaya seeds for the dressing.

Dice the avocado and papaya flesh and place in a mixing bowl. Add the crayfish, spring onion/scallion and salt and pepper to taste.

Put all the ingredients for the papaya seed dressing into a blender and blitz until well blended. The papaya seeds should be broken down enough so that they look like little flecks of cracked black pepper.

Pour the papaya seed dressing over everything to taste and toss so everything is nicely coated (keeping any leftovers in a jar in the fridge).

Pull a leaf from a lettuce head and put a large heaped spoonful of the crayfish mixture on top. Repeat until you have used all of the mixture.

Garnish with a few macadamia halves on each lettuce cup and serve immediately with lime wedges.

TIP
This is also tasty made with cooked prawns/shrimp instead of crayfish and with mango instead of papaya.

As an alternative to lettuce cups, you can also make little wonton cups by pressing wonton wrappers into lightly greased muffin pan cups and baking for about 8 minutes, or until golden – see the wonton packet for oven temperature, but it's usually around 180°C (350°F) Gas 4.

HAWAIIAN-STYLE RIBS

Halfway between Seoul, in Korea, and Kansas City, Missouri is... you've guessed it, Hawai'i. Being at the geographical midpoint, almost a culinary crossroads, between these two places could explain this style of cooking. Not really exotic or tropical or even fusion of sorts, but just a straightforward adoption of these cooking styles. Here are two of the most popular recipes. One for KC-Hawaiian baby back ribs, the other for Korean Kalbi, beef short ribs. Follow the methods closely to produce ribs that will set the benchmark. They are great grilled/broiled at home and taken on a 'tailgate', or serve with some sides for a proper Lū'au.

KALBI RIBS

This is a very easy, forgiving recipe provided you have the right cut of meat. Hopefully you can source the ribs from a Korean or Asian market, or try asking your butcher to prepare them for you. If you have short ribs, here's how to prepare them.

SERVES 4

500 g/1 lb. 2 oz. short ribs, on the
  bone, cut crossways or Korean style
Little Gem/Bibb lettuce, to serve
3 spring onions/scallions, finely sliced,
  to serve
sesame seeds, to garnish

FOR THE MARINADE

2 kiwis, peeled and mashed
3 tablespoons fresh pineapple juice
2 tablespoons rice wine vinegar
3 tablespoons light soy sauce
1 tablespoon dark soy sauce
2 tablespoons sesame oil
3 tablespoons sugar
2 tablespoons sesame seeds
6 garlic cloves, crushed
4 banana shallots, grated
2 teaspoons freshly ground black
  pepper

First freeze the meat for 20 minutes or so. Lay out a rib on a board, bone side down, and carefully open it up by making a lateral cut just above the bone but don't slice all the way through the meat. Make another cut, again not all the way through, opening up the meat. Repeat the process until you have a piece of meat approx. 1-cm/½-inch thick attached to the bone at one end. Flatten the meat out. Repeat the process with the remaining ribs.

Mix all the marinade ingredients together. In a large metal tray, spread out the ribs and rub in half the marinade. Leave for at least 1 hour.

Prepare a charcoal grill. When the coals are ready, move to one side of the grill. Place the meat on the hot side of the grill and baste with the remaining marinade. Turn once and baste again. Cook for at least 4 minutes for medium-rare, or longer if desired. If the outside of the meat is burning and the inside is too raw, move it to cooler part of the grill.

Serve on lettuce leaves with spring onions/scallions and more sesame seeds as garnish.

Serve with Red Chilli Salsa (see page 133) or Gochujang paste. Good with Sticky Aubergine Poke (see page 32).

KANSAS CITY-HAWAIIAN BACK RIBS

Huli-Huli literally means 'turn turn' in Hawaiian, referring to the fact that the meat is repeatedly turned and basted. Here, huli huli also refers to the marinade used in this island style teriyaki sauce. It is great combined with a Kansas City-style rub.

SERVES 3

1.5–2 kg/3¼–4½ lb. or 2 large racks
of baby back ribs

FOR THE RUB

1 tablespoon cumin seeds
2 tablespoons coriander seeds
150 g/¾ cup brown sugar
4 tablespoons Spanish paprika
1 tablespoon freshly ground black
  pepper
1 tablespoon cayenne pepper
3 garlic cloves, mashed

FOR THE HULI-HULI SAUCE

150 g/¾ cup light brown sugar
120 ml/½ cup light soy sauce
150 ml/⅔ cup pineapple juice
1½ teaspoons sesame oil
½ teaspoon dried chilli/hot red pepper
  flakes
6 garlic cloves, finely chopped
5–7.5-cm/2–3-inch piece of fresh
  ginger, peeled and finely chopped

For the rub, lightly toast the cumin and coriander seeds in a hot frying pan/skillet. Finely grind the seeds using a pestle and mortar. Add the remaining rub ingredients and mix well.

Place the ribs in a metal tray and coat evenly with the rub. Let them rest for at least 30 minutes, but no longer than an hour.

Meanwhile, make the Huli-Huli Sauce. Place all the ingredients together in a bowl and mix well. Use some for marinating the ribs, some for basting during cooking and reserve some for serving.

If smoking the ribs, allow at least 4 hours with the smoker temperature at around 110°C (225°F). Start with the ribs uncovered for 2 hours, then cover in foil for an hour, and uncover for the last hour. The last hour is when you apply the Huli-Huli Sauce in several layers until done.

If oven cooking, preheat the oven to 160°C (325°F) Gas 3. Cover a roasting pan in foil, making a crease at the outer edges. Place the ribs, curved side down, on the foil, carefully cover with more foil and cook for 1½ hours. Now remove the foil, turn the ribs up the other way and baste with pan juices and Huli-Huli Sauce. Cook for 30 minutes, then turn the ribs over and baste again. Cook for another 30 minutes and continue basting until cooked. Check the meat is tender all the way through by testing with a knife. Finally, turn the grill/broiler to its highest setting, turn the ribs with the meatier side up and brown for 3 minutes.

Serve the ribs with the reserved Huli-Huli Sauce. On the side, have some Red Chilli Salsa (see page 133) and Pineapple-Red Chilli Salsa (see page 134).

SIDES, SALSAS &
SAUCES

PACIFIC PANTRY FILLERS & MORE.

'ULU (BREADFRUIT) MASH

A large, lumpy looking fruit from the South Pacific, mashed ulu is a popular Hawaiian alternative to potato mash. I add garlic and butter, just like Aunties do.

SERVES 6

1 large breadfruit*
3 garlic cloves, peeled
1 tablespoon salt, plus more to taste
butter, to taste
chopped chives, to garnish
cracked black pepper

* This should be green and mature and just soft to the touch, but not too soft. Use it on the day of purchase as breadfruit ripen quickly and will be too sweet by the following day. If buying in advance, get one that is green and mature but still firm and wait for it to soften slightly.

Peel the breadfruit with a sharp knife. Slice in half lengthways and remove the core. Chop the breadfruit into 2.5-cm/1-inch cubes.

Bring a large pan of water to the boil. Add the breadfruit, garlic and salt. Boil for approx. 20 minutes, until the breadfruit is tender. Drain the breadfruit and garlic and place in a large mixing bowl.

Add some butter and start mashing – breadfruit is firmer than potatoes so put some effort in. Add a little boiling water, as necessary, until you have a smooth, mashed potato consistency. Top with a small knob/pat of butter and sprinkle with chopped chives and cracked black pepper.

Serve immediately as a Pacific alternative to mashed potatoes.

TIP
For a dairy-free/vegan version, replace the butter with good olive oil. You can also brown some shallots and/or sliced mushrooms and add them to the mash.

MISO TENDERSTEM BROCCOLI

With a nod to Japan, the miso paste transforms this family favourite into something a bit more out of the ordinary.

SERVES 4

400 g/14 oz. tenderstem broccoli/broccolini
4 tablespoons sesame seeds
1 tablespoon light soy sauce
1 tablespoon chinkiang vinegar (Chinese black rice vinegar)
1 teaspoon runny honey
1 teaspoon ketjap manis
½ teaspoon sesame oil
2 tablespoons miso paste (I like to use white)
1 red chilli/chile, sliced

Steam the broccoli/broccolini for 3–4 minutes.

Toast the sesame seeds in a dry pan until golden, then grind three-quarters into dust using a pestle and mortar.

Combine the soy, vinegar, honey, kecap manis, sesame oil and miso paste, giving it a quick whizz in a blender.

Arrange the broccoli on a plate, garnish with the remaining sesame seeds and the thinly sliced red chilli/chile. Serve the sauce as a dipping sauce.

SESAME GREEN BEANS

As you've probably noticed, the flavours of sesame and soy are very prevalent in Hawaiian cooking. The seeds give a great little crunch to classic green beans.

SERVES 4

500 g/1 lb. 2 oz. thin French
  green beans
2 tablespoons sesame seeds
3 tablespoons dark soy sauce

Remove the tops from the beans. Lightly steam them, then refresh in cold water so they keep their colour and crunch.

Slice the beans on the diagonal into 2-cm/¾-inch pieces. Toast the sesame seeds in a dry pan until slightly golden, then grind lightly using a pestle and mortar.

Lightly coat the beans in the soy sauce and then toss in the sesame seeds.

SUNSHINE CORN WITH CHILLI BUTTER

One of my favourites, this dish takes me right back to Southern California – hand-picking my fresh corn in the farmers' market before cooking it over an oak barbecue.

SERVES 4

4 whole corn on the cob,
  in their husks
a good knob/pat of butter
small bunch of coriander/cilantro,
  chopped
½ teaspoon cayenne pepper
good pinch of salt
squeeze of fresh lime juice

Remove the first outer layer of each corn husk. Barbecue or oven cook in a preheated oven at 200°C (400°F) Gas 6 until soft – this will take approx. 35 minutes, depending on the size of the corn.

Remove the remaining husks from the corn, then toast in a dry griddle pan until you achieve the desired level of burntness.

Meanwhile, melt the butter in a pan over a low heat, combine with the chopped coriander/cilantro and the cayenne pepper.

Smother the corn in the butter mixture, sprinkle with salt from a height and a squeeze of lime juice, then serve.

TIP
Also good served with a teaspoon of SB Red Salsa (see page 135) or ancho chilli/chili sauce.

YUZU-MANGO SALSA

*This is the salsa we turn to for our salmon poke.
It ticks all the boxes: light, fresh, tart and, above
all, perfect with salmon.*

SERVES 4

2 ripe mangoes, peeled and stoned
3 spring onions/scallions
2 small red chillies/chiles
2 tablespoons yuzu juice
4 tablespoons apple juice

Cut half into small dice, and put the other half into
a blender with the spring onions/scallions, chillies/
chiles, and yuzu and apple juices. Blitz until fairly
smooth. Mix together with the diced mango.

TOMATILLO SALSA

*Found in California and Mexico, this mild salsa
works very nicely with tacos and nachos.*

SERVES 4

6 tomatillos, dehusked
freshly squeezed juice of 1 lime
2 garlic cloves, peeled
1 onion
pinch of salt
generous handful of coriander/cilantro

Preheat a dry cast iron pan. Put the dehusked
tomatillos in to lightly char on the surface – you
are not trying to cook them through. Put the
tomatillos in a blender with the lime juice, garlic,
onion, salt, and coriander/cilantro and whizz up.
Add some water if it's too thick.

BURNT CORN SALSA

*This is a firm favourite with our customers at Island Poké. The charred, zingy
corn provides an additional layer of flavour and texture to any poke bowl.*

SERVES 3

2 corn on the cob, or 250 g/2 cups
    frozen sweetcorn/corn kernels
freshly squeezed juice of 1 lime
2 red chillies/chiles, finely chopped
1 sweet white onion, finely chopped
handful of coriander/cilantro,
    chopped
2 tablespoons olive oil
salt and freshly ground black pepper

cook's blowtorch

If using fresh corn, heat up a cast iron griddle pan until
quite hot and keep the heat on. Remove the husks and
place the corn in the pan. Turn so all sides show charring.
When ready, and not necessarily cooked through, stand
each corn on end and run a knife down the cob on all sides
to remove the kernels. Spread out on a baking sheet.

If using frozen corn, bring a pan of water to the boil.
Add the corn and boil for 5 minutes. Drain and spread.

Light the blowtorch and carefully char the top surfaces
of the sweetorn/corn kernels on the baking sheet. Just do
this on a single side of the corn rather than all round.

Put the lime juice, chillies/chiles, onion, coriander/
cilantro and the corn into a serving bowl and combine.
Drizzle over the olive oil. Add salt and pepper to taste.

RED CHILLI SALSA

When you think of a classic salsa made of dried chillies/chiles that all have a great depth of flavour, such as Ancho, Pasilla and Chile Negro, this is the one. Chillies/chiles have distinctive characters that range from a dried prune and raisin aroma to nutty and smoky, and these flavours are greatly enhanced when the chillies/chiles are slightly charred. There's no set rule for the combination of chillies/chiles that go into this salsa, but it is traditional to use a variety to give complexity, not just heat. This salsa should feature as the centrepiece in any spread and is good accompanied by a contrasting fresh-tasting Pico de Gallo (see page 134).

SERVES 6

6 flavourful Mexican dried chillies/
   chiles, such as Ancho, Pasilla,
   Chile Negro, Guajillo, New Mexico
4 small hot dried chillies/chiles, such
   as Pequin, Thai, Chipotle
150 g/1 cup sultanas/golden raisins
   or prunes (optional)

Lightly toast all the chillies/chiles in a dry cast iron frying pan/skillet, taking care not to burn them.

Bring a large pan of water to the boil, then turn the heat down to a light simmer and immerse the chillies/chiles. Simmer for 10 minutes or so, then turn off the heat and leave the chillies/chiles to rehydrate for at least an hour. You may need to weigh down the chillies/chiles to keep them submerged.

When rehydrated, remove the stems and put the chillies/chiles into a blender with a little of the pan water and blitz to a salsa consistency. Add a little more water if too dry.

If you want a fruitier salsa, add some sultanas/golden raisins or dried prunes to the rehydrating process and blitz with the chillies/chiles.

PICO DE GALLO

This is the most basic, versatile and refreshing salsa, found pretty much everywhere from So-Cal down through Baja and Mexico. It is ideally suited to being splashed over tacos of any description and served alongside ceviches and pokes. Consider it the ideal companion or contrast to any salsa made with rehydrated chillies/chiles, or tomatillos. I have found myself finishing off bowls of Pico de Gallo like munching through a salad, so moreish.

SERVES 3

handful of coriander/cilantro
4 tomatoes
1 white onion, preferably
  a sweet variety
1 jalapeño
freshly squeezed juice of 1 lime
salt

Roughly chop the coriander/cilantro and tomatoes. Finely chop the onion and jalapeño. Mix together in a serving bowl and add lime juice and salt to taste.

PINEAPPLE-RED CHILLI SALSA

This is the salsa we use day in, day out and it's a firm favourite with our customers. It acts as a tart flavour bomb over poke, but is equally useful with fish tacos, and in many Hawaiian dishes. The flavours are best when this is made and served fresh.

SERVES 4

1 medium fresh pineapple
1½ white onions
2 red chillies/chiles
freshly squeezed juice of 1 lime
salt

Peel, core and dice the fresh pineapple. Finely chop the onions and chillies/chiles. Mix together in a serving bowl and add a little lime juice and salt to taste.

SB RED SALSA

Almost a cross between Hawaiian chilli/chile pepper water and a Mexican hot sauce such as Cholulla, this is the best thing to go along with anything from quesadillas and fish tacos to swirling over a ceviche. One of my favourite restaurants in Santa Barbara uses it liberally over their version of Agua Chilli Shrimp (see page 35) – a dish I go back to just for this salsa. Try making up a decent amount to keep in the fridge for instant satisfaction.

SERVES 6

6 long red chillies/chiles
3 garlic cloves, peeled
1 tablespoon cumin seeds
400-g/14-oz. can whole
   Italian tomatoes
salt

Heat up a cast iron pan until fairly hot. Dry toast the chillies/chiles in the pan until lightly charred on all sides. Toast the garlic in the pan at the same time. Set aside.

Dry toast the cumin seeds in a small pan until they take on a little colour, but watch they don't burn. Grind the seeds using a pestle and mortar.

Put everything in a blender along with the tomatoes and whizz until you have a smooth purée. Add salt to taste. Allow to cool and stir in some water to loosen the salsa until you have an easy drizzling consistency.

Store in bottles, as with the Kalua Chipotle Ketchup (see page 136), or store in the fridge and use within 1 week.

TERIYAKI SAUCE

Originally from Japan, Hawai'i has adopted teriyaki as its own. The sauce should have a syrupy consistency and a comfortingly sweet but savoury taste. It is frequently used in chicken, salmon and beef dishes, but can dress up noodles, rice or vegetables or be used as a dipping sauce. The cornflour/cornstarch is just used to thicken the consistency of the sauce, so omit if you want to use it as a marinade.

**MAKES APPROX.
350 ML/SCANT 1½ CUPS**

120 ml/½ cup soy sauce
1½ tablespoons honey
1½ teaspoons minced fresh ginger
1 teaspoon minced fresh garlic
2 tablespoons mirin
4 tablespoons demerara/turbinado
   sugar
2 tablespoons cornflour/cornstarch

Combine all ingredients, except the cornflour/cornstarch, in a pan. Add 60 ml/¼ cup water and warm gently; do not boil.

Mix the cornflour/cornstarch with 3 tablespoons cold water to make a liquid paste. Whisk this into the sauce until dissolved. Heat gently, stirring frequently, until the sauce begins to thicken to a syrupy consistency, then remove from the heat (the sauce will continue to thicken as it cools). If the sauce is too thick, add a little more water to loosen it.

Store in a sterilized sealed jar in the refrigerator and use within 1 month.

For a tropical twist, substitute the water with the same quantity of pineapple juice.

KALUA CHIPOTLE KETCHUP

This Mexican inspired sauce has everything you want, with heat and a deep smoky undertone, it will transform anything it touches. Also makes a great BBQ marinade.

**MAKES 4 X 150-ML/5-OZ.
BOTTLES**

3 x 400-g/14-oz. cans whole
   Italian tomatoes
3 tablespoons dark soy sauce
3 tablespoons muscovado sugar
1 teaspoon fish sauce
1 tablespoon mirin
3 tablespoons chipotle paste

Put the whole tomatoes in a saucepan and heat gently. Add the soy sauce, muscovado sugar, fish sauce and mirin. Stir and bring the mixture to a very low simmer. Add in the chipotle paste and stir together. Continue to simmer for approx. 30 minutes until slightly reduced. Put everything in a blender and whizz to a smooth purée.

Sterilize the bottles by putting them in a boiling water bath, or microwave. When the bottles are ready, pour in the warm sauce and close the seals or lids. Store in a dry place, out of the light. Once open, keep the bottle in the fridge and use within one week.

CHIPOTLE CREMA

*A creamy, milder version of the chipotle
ketchup, this one works on anything.*

SERVES 4

1 tablespoon Kalua Chipotle Ketchup
(see page 136) or chipotle paste
3 tablespoons double/heavy cream
1 tablespoon good-quality mayonnaise

Mix the ingredients together in a bowl.

CRISPY SHALLOTS

*The textural hero of the poke bowl, these
crispy fried onions add an irresistible crunch.*

**MAKES APPROX.
350 ML/SCANT 1½ CUPS**

4 shallots, finely sliced
vegetable oil
3 tablespoons plain/all-purpose flour

Shallow-fry the onions in a little oil
over a medium heat for 5 minutes.
Using a slotted spoon, remove the
onions from the oil and drain on paper
towels. Add a light coating of flour to
the onions. Return the onions to the
oil over a high heat and fry for about
1 minute again until golden.

PICKLES

*The ingredients that helps define the new types of poke from their
more traditional Hawaiian roots are these punchy pickles, used
as quirky garnishes. There are some fairly subtle pickles, and some
that stretch the boundaries. In most cases they are used to enhance
or balance flavours or as a palate cleanser. In the Hawaiian
context, pickles should be more accurately termed 'preserved
vegetables' as they are closer to the Japanese tsukemono
than western-style pickles. It is best to put your
Japanese culinary hat on and consider balance,
ceremony and especially fragrance.*

CUCUMBER PICKLES

SERVES 6

2 cucumbers
1 tablespoon salt
120 g/4 oz. hijiki or arame
   seaweed
235 ml/1 cup rice wine
   vinegar
180 g/scant 1 cup granulated
   sugar
1 teaspoon black sesame
   seeds

Slice the cucumbers on the diagonal and spread out on a ceramic platter. Mix the salt into the cucumber. Let stand for 10 minutes, then rinse and pat dry.

Place the seaweed in a small bowl and hydrate in a little warm water for 10 minutes, then drain and squeeze out the excess water.

Combine the vinegar and sugar in a medium saucepan with 235 ml/1 cup water and bring to the boil. Take off the heat and add the cucumber, seaweed and sesame seeds. Place in a sealable container, making sure the liquid is covering the cucumber, cool down, then refrigerate.

Try to let the flavours mellow for a few days before eating. Consume within 1 month.

PICKLED SCOTCH BONNETS

MAKES ENOUGH TO FILL A 1-LITRE/1-QUART PRESERVING JAR

500 ml/2¼ cups vinegar – can be
   half white wine vinegar and half
   red wine vinegar
2 tablespoons sugar
2 teaspoons salt
1 teaspoon allspice berries
280 g/10 oz. Scotch Bonnets

Prepare the pickling solution. Place the vinegar, sugar and salt in a medium pan with 120 ml/ ½ cup water and boil until the sugar has dissolved. Add the allspice berries.

Carefully cut the tops off the Scotch Bonnets to expose the inside of the peppers to the pickling solution. Place the peppers in a second pan with enough water to cover and bring gently to the boil for no more than 1 minute. Strain the peppers and pack into the jar. Pour over the slightly cooled pickling solution, leaving a 1-cm/ ½-inch gap at the top. Seal.

Try to let it rest for a few days before using to allow the flavours to blend. Will keep for many months stored in the refrigerator.

TIP
When handling Scotch Bonnets, wear gloves and make sure you do not rub your eyes.

PICKLED GINGER

MAKES ENOUGH TO FILL A 500-ML/17-OZ. PRESERVING JAR

250 g/9 oz. fresh ginger –
   try using young ginger
1 tablespoon sea salt flakes
60 g/5 tablespoons sugar
300 ml/1¼ cups rice wine vinegar
3 tablespoons water
2 drops red food colouring
   (optional) (see Tip)

Peel the ginger and slice thinly. Pile into a bowl and rub in the salt. Cover and refrigerate for at least 2 hours. Squeeze the ginger to remove the salt and the liquid, then place the ginger in the preserving jar.

Bring the remaining ingredients to a simmer in a small pan. Make sure the sugar is dissolved. Pour into the jar and cool a little before sealing.

Try to leave undisturbed for at least three days before using. This allows the flavours to mellow and the ginger to have less kick.

TIP
If you can source the youngest possible ginger, it will naturally turn pale pink in the pickling process. Otherwise, add a drop or two of red food colouring into the marinade.

PICKLED SHIITAKES

MAKES ENOUGH TO FILL A 1-LITRE/1-QUART PRESERVING JAR

100 g/3½ oz. dried shiitake
    mushrooms
1 small piece of fresh ginger,
    peeled and cut into thin batons
350 ml/scant 1½ cups dark soy
    sauce
350 ml/scant 1½ cups rice wine
    vinegar
250 g/1¼ cups granulated sugar

Boil enough water to nearly fill
a medium-sized pan. Place the
mushrooms in the pan and cover
with the boiling water. Cover
the mushrooms with a plate that
can be weighted to keep them
submerged. Leave the mushrooms
in the water to soak for at least
15 minutes.

Drain, but save at least 250 ml/
1 cup plus 1 tablespoon of the
soaking liquid.

Place all the remaining
ingredients with the mushrooms
and reserved water back in the
pan and stir to combine.

Bring to the boil. Reduce the
heat to low and simmer, uncovered,
for 30 minutes, stirring from time
to time. Take the pan off the heat
and let the ingredients cool.

Place in the preserving jar
and refrigerate for at least 2 days
before using. Can be kept
refrigerated for up to 2 weeks.

PICKLED MANGO

MAKES ENOUGH TO FILL TWO 500-ML/17-OZ. PRESERVING JARS

1 kg/2¼ lb. green mangoes
10 seedless li hing mui
    (salty dried plums)
4 red chillies/chiles, sliced
    in half lengthways
500 ml/2 cups plus 2 tablespoons
    apple cider vinegar
250 g/1¼ cups granulated sugar
60 g/¼ cup salt

Peel, stone and slice the mangoes
into spears. Place in the jars with
the li hing mui and chillies/chiles.

Combine the vinegar, sugar
and salt in a medium saucepan
and bring to the boil to dissolve
the sugar and salt. Remove from
the heat and leave to cool slightly.

Pour over the mango spears
and cover. When cooled,
refrigerate. Try not to open for
at least a day to allow the flavours
to blend. This will keep for up to
1 year in a dry, dark place.

TIP
Li hing mui, or salty dried
plums is available from most
Asian supermarkets. Green
mango can be sourced from
most supermarkets as underripe
mango. Try not to buy mangoes
that are going ripe.

PINEAPPLE & CUCUMBER KIMCHI

MAKES ENOUGH TO FILL TWO 475-ML/16-OZ. PRESERVING JARS

2 medium cucumbers
2 tablespoons sea salt flakes
1 pineapple, not too ripe, peeled, cored,
    diced into 2.5-cm/1-inch pieces
1 green mango, peeled, stoned and
    sliced into 5-cm/2-inch strips
3 spring onions/scallions, diced

FOR THE MARINADE
½ Asian pear, peeled, cored
    and cut into chunks
3 tablespoons Korean red chilli/
    chili powder
1½ tablespoons fish sauce
2 tablespoons rice wine vinegar
2 teaspoons freshly grated ginger
4 garlic cloves, finely chopped
2½ teaspoons granulated sugar

Slice the cucumbers into quarters
lengthways, then into 2.5-cm/
1-inch pieces. Place in a stainless
steel bowl, sprinkle with the salt
and set aside for 20 minutes.
Rinse in water, then set to drain.

Blend the marinade ingredients
until smooth. Add the pineapple,
mango, spring onions/scallions
and drained cucumber to a bowl.
Add the marinade and stir well.
Divide between the jars, including
any leftover marinade, and cover
with lids. Leave at room
temperature for 12 hours, then
refrigerate for 24–48 hours
before eating. Kimchi lasts for
2–3 weeks in the refrigerator.

TROPICAL TREATS &
TEMPTING TIPPLES

ISLAND DELIGHTS TO KEEP YOU SMILING
FROM SUNRISE TO SUNSET.

HAUPIA MACADAMIA PIE

Haupia is classic Hawaiian coconut custard. It's usually cold set, cut into squares and presented on a ti leaf, served as the dessert part of a plate lunch or at a luau. One of my favourite ways to make haupia is in a pie form and this particular combo, on a biscuit/cookie crumb crust topped with caramelized macadamia nuts, is always a winner.

SERVES 8

FOR THE CRUST
250 g/9 oz. digestive biscuits/
   graham crackers
170 g/¾ cup butter, melted
100 g/½ cup caster/superfine sugar

FOR THE HAUPIA FILLING
75 g/¾ cup cornflour/cornstarch
400-ml/14-fl oz. can coconut milk
100 g/½ cup caster/superfine sugar

FOR THE TOPPING
100 g/3½ oz. caramelized or honey-
   roasted macadamia nuts, crushed

*23-cm/9-inch round pie pan, greased
with coconut oil and base lined with
baking parchment*

Preheat the oven to 190°C (375°F) Gas 5.

Put the biscuits/crackers in a clean, sealed polythene bag and roll with a rolling pin, or alternatively blitz in a food processor, into a breadcrumb consistency. Tip into a bowl, pour in the melted butter and sugar and mix well. Press the mixture into the greased and lined pie pan and bake in the preheated oven for 10 minutes or until golden brown and just toasted. Set aside to cool.

For the haupia filling, mix the cornflour/cornstarch with 235 ml/1 cup water and set aside. Place the coconut milk and sugar in a pan with 120 ml/½ cup water and bring to the boil over a high heat. Pour the cornflour/cornstarch mixture into the boiling coconut milk and cook over a medium heat, whisking continuously until the mixture thickens. When the mixture is smooth and thick, pour evenly over the pie crust. Cool to room temperature, then chill in the refrigerator until cold.

Top with the crushed caramelized or honey-roasted macadamia nuts just before serving.

TIP
Add a layer of sliced bananas to the pie crust before pouring the haupia custard on top to set. Top with whipped cream and the crushed macadamias.

Switch out the digestive biscuits/graham crackers for your favourite biscuits/cookies – I've tried Hobnobs and Oreos and they were both yummy.

BLUEBERRY BANANA PORRIDGE SQUARES

These make a good alternative to breakfast bars and are a cross between a bowl of porridge and a flapjack. Apart from the maple syrup, which you can substitute with apple juice or your preferred sweetener, this is a guilt-free grab-and-go snack which tastes like a comforting treat but is actually pretty healthy!

MAKES 6–8

300 g/3 cups jumbo/old-fashioned oats
250 g/2 cups blueberries
½ banana, peeled
225 ml/scant 1 cup oat milk
1½ teaspoons vanilla powder
115 ml/½ cup maple syrup
150 g/1½ cups pecans

20 x 30-cm/8 x 12-inch cake pan, greased with a small amount of coconut oil and lined with baking parchment

Preheat the oven to 180°C (350°F) Gas 4.

Put the oats, 125 g/1 cup of the blueberries, the banana, milk, vanilla powder and maple syrup into a food processor. Pulse until just combined (but not fine). Tip the mixture into a bowl. Stir in half the remaining blueberries.

Roughly chop 100 g/1 cup of the pecans and stir into the mixture. Reserve the remaining 50 g/½ cup unchopped nuts for the top.

Spoon the mixture into the cake pan spreading it evenly. Scatter the top with the remaining blueberries and pecans. Bake in the preheated oven for 15–20 minutes, until lightly golden and cooked through. Let cool and cut into squares.

TIP
Try adding raisins, pecans, strawberries or desiccated/dried shredded coconut, reducing the blueberry/banana quantities accordingly.

NANA'S NANA BREAD

This is one of those warm, comforting classics. Aunties (and nanas!) in Hawai'i typically have their own versions of it and it's hardly ever made with the same quantities or ingredients twice. It's a very forgiving recipe, so you can have a play around with different fruit, vegetables, nuts and seeds and come up with your own signature combination!

MAKES 2 LOAVES

390 g/3 cups wholemeal/wholewheat flour

200 g/1 cup granulated sugar (white or golden), plus 2 teaspoons for sprinkling

1 teaspoon salt

¾ teaspoon baking powder

1 teaspoon bicarbonate of soda/ baking soda

1 teaspoon ground cinnamon

2 eggs, lightly beaten

235 ml/1 cup sunflower/safflower oil

2 teaspoons vanilla extract (or the seeds from 1 vanilla pod/bean)

400 g/2 cups mashed banana

200 g/7 oz. unsalted macadamia nuts, crushed (pecans are another favourite)

200 g/1¼ cups dried cranberries

2 x 900-g/2-lb loaf pans, greased with coconut oil

Preheat the oven to 160°C (325°F) Gas 3.

Put the flour, sugar, salt, baking powder, bicarbonate of soda/baking soda and cinnamon into a large mixing bowl and stir well to mix.

In a separate bowl, combine the eggs, oil and vanilla, then add them to the dry ingredients, stirring while you add. When blended to a breadcrumb consistency, add in the mashed bananas and roughly stir (you don't want to totally liquify them) until you have a thick batter consistency. Stir in the nuts and cranberries.

Divide the mixture between the two greased loaf pans. Sprinkle a teaspoon of sugar on top of each loaf and place in the centre of the preheated oven. Bake for 1 hour or until a cocktail stick/toothpick inserted in the centre comes out clean.

Leave to stand in the loaf pans for 5 minutes, then turn out onto a wire rack to cool. Slice and serve as is, or toast (this is probably best done under the grill/broiler, rather than in a toaster) and serve buttered.

TIP

You can substitute the banana with the same quantity of grated raw courgettes/zucchini and even add chocolate chips. You can also try substituting the cranberries with desiccated/dried shredded coconut or other dried fruit, such as chopped mango or raisins.

GRANDMA BETSY'S COCOA MOCHI

Mochi is a Japanese sweet treat typically made from rice flour, sugar and a flavouring. It has a soft, chewy, glutinous texture. This particular mochi recipe is one of my Aunty Jo's signature dishes which she inherited from her mother, Grandma Betsy, and has kindly allowed us to share. This mochi is a bit cakier than others, and it has always been a treat I look forward to at our family gatherings.

MAKES 24

285 g/2½ cups mochiko rice flour, plus extra for dusting
350 g/1¾ cups caster/superfine sugar
3 tablespoons unsweetened cocoa powder, plus extra for dusting
1 tablespoon bicarbonate of soda/baking soda
2 eggs
340-g/12-oz. can evaporated milk
340-g/12-oz. can coconut milk
60 g/¼ cup butter, melted and cooled
2 teaspoons vanilla extract
icing/confectioners' sugar, for dusting

23 x 33 x 5-cm/9 x 13 x 2-inch cake pan, greased with either butter or coconut oil and lined with baking parchment

Preheat the oven to 180°C (350°F) Gas 4.

Sift the dry ingredients together in a large mixing bowl. Set aside.

Lightly beat the eggs in a jug/pitcher, then add the evaporated milk, coconut milk, melted butter and vanilla essence. Pour the wet ingredients into the dry ones and mix until smooth.

Pour the mixture into the greased and lined cake pan and bake in the preheated oven for 1 hour or until a cocktail stick/toothpick inserted in the centre comes out clean. It should be more dry than gooey in the middle.

Cool completely in the pan, then dust with a little cocoa powder, icing/confectioners' sugar and mochiko flour and cut into squares or rectangles.

HAWAIIAN MALASADAS

These are an adaption of a Portuguese recipe – a light, fluffy cube dusted with sugar and stuffed with an intensely flavoured filling. In Honolulu, Leonard's Bakery holds the distinction of making the best, but this is our version you can try for yourself. Choose between a delicious guava compote or a yuzu custard filling.

MAKES ABOUT 24

FOR THE MALASADAS
3 large eggs
70 g/5 tablespoons/⅔ stick unsalted butter, at room temperature
150 g/¾ cup granulated sugar, plus extra for dusting
1 teaspoon salt
700 g/5½ cups plain/all-purpose flour, plus extra for dusting
2 x 7 g/¼ oz. sachets of easy blend/ active dried yeast
235 ml/1 cup just-boiled water
90 ml/⅓ cup evaporated milk
2 teaspoons vanilla extract
vegetable oil, for deep frying

FOR THE GUAVA COMPOTE
475 ml/2 cups guava juice
2 eggs
2 egg yolks
2 tablespoons sugar
30 g/¼ stick unsalted butter, softened

Put 1 egg, the butter, sugar and salt in an electric stand mixer. Using the dough hook, blend together well. Add 650 g/5 cups of flour and the yeast. Beat together for a minute. Add the just-boiled water, evaporated milk and vanilla extract and beat until well blended. Beat in the remaining 2 eggs, then add the remaining 50 g/½ cup of flour and beat until the dough starts to come away from the sides of the bowl. If necessary, add a little more flour to reduce stickiness and beat for another 10 minutes.

Form the dough into a ball, then cover the bowl in clingfilm/ plastic wrap. Leave to rise for at least 2 hours at room temperature or overnight in the fridge until doubled in size.

When risen, punch the dough down and cut into two pieces. On a floured surface, roll out one of the pieces to a rectangle approx. 40 x 30 cm/ 16 x 12 inches, about 1-cm/½-inch thick. Cut lengthways into three strips. Cut each strip crossways into approx. 4 x 5-cm/2-inch squares. Repeat with the other piece. Put the squares on the lined baking sheets, loosely cover in clingfilm/plastic wrap and let rise again until doubled in size.

Meanwhile, make the guava compote. Place the guava juice in a heavy-based pan, bring to the boil, then simmer for about 30 minutes until reduced down to 120 ml/½ cup. It should be quite syrupy. Pour into a medium bowl; set aside to cool completely.

When the guava syrup is completely cold, whisk in the eggs, yolks, sugar and half the butter. Using a double-boiler, cook over a very low heat, constantly whisking, until a curd starts to form and starts to stick to the bottom of the bowl. This could take 25–30 minutes. Continue to cook on a very low heat while whisking until volcanic bubbles form, continue for just a minute, then remove from the heat. Stir in the remaining butter. Cover with clingfilm/plastic wrap directly on the compote surface. Chill.

Make the yuzu custard by beating the egg yolks with half the milk. Add the sugar and flour and mix very well together making sure there are no lumps. In a small pan, bring the remaining milk

FOR THE YUZU CUSTARD

4 egg yolks

400 ml/1⅔ cups whole milk

120 g/generous ½ cup caster/
   superfine sugar

50 g/heaped ⅓ cup tablespoons plain/
   all-purpose flour

60–70 g/2¼–2½ oz. good-quality
   white chocolate, roughly chopped

2 tablespoons yuzu juice

2 baking sheets, lined with baking
   parchment
2 piping/pastry bags

to a gentle simmer, then pour into the egg mixture, whisking vigorously. Pass through a sieve back into the pan and stir over a medium heat until the custard thickens. Remove from the heat.

Place the white chocolate into a double-boiler and melt (or melt gently in a microwave). Add the melted chocolate and yuzu juice to the custard and gently mix together. Pour the custard into a clean bowl. Cover by placing clingfilm/plastic wrap directly on the custard surface to prevent a skin from forming and chill.

To cook the malasadas, into a large pan, pour oil to a depth of 4 cm/1½ inches and heat to 180°C (350°F). Alternatively, use a deep-fat fryer. Using a slotted spoon, gently drop in one or two at a time and fry until golden-brown, turning once, for about 2 minutes on each side. Transfer to a plate lined with paper towels to drain. Cool until just warm, then generously sprinkle with granulated sugar. The malasadas will be quite crisp when they first come out of the fryer, but should soften when cooled.

Fill the malasadas with the compote or custard of your choice by making a small incision in one side with a skewer or chopstick, creating a hole for the filling. Put the fillings into separate piping/pastry bags and fill each malasada until you can see the sides start to expand. Best eaten on the day they are made.

MANGO & GINGER CHIA POTS

*This dish turns the ordinary chia seed into a tropical flavour sensation
that is as kind to your body as it is to your tastebuds.*

MAKES 4

60 g/2¼ oz. chia seeds

200 ml/¾ cup apple juice, plus
   2 tablespoons

150 g/5½ oz. mango flesh, plus extra
   to decorate

50 g/3½ tablespoons cashew nut
   butter

10 g/¼ oz. stem ginger

toasted coconut, to decorate

Soak the chia seeds in 200 ml/¾ cup of the apple juice overnight.

The next day, blitz the mango, nut butter and stem ginger together, then loosen with the remaining 2 tablespoons apple juice.

Add the soaked chia seeds and mix everything together well, then spoon into four serving bowls or glasses. Decorate with toasted coconut and mango cubes.

PINEAPPLE CORNBREAD MUFFINS

Although not really a traditional Hawaiian recipe, these lovely golden muffins combine flavours from the Pacific Rim and were too good not to include. They have a subtle cornbread texture infused with a tropical hint of pineapple. The apple sauce, pineapple juice and coconut milk keep them moist without taking away from their fluffy moreishness. They also happen to be vegan so are a good option if you need a milk- or egg-free recipe, or if you want an allergen-friendly option for parties. There are no nuts either and the wheat flour can easily be substituted with a gluten-free version.

MAKES 12

150 g/1 cup polenta/cornmeal
260 g/2 cups wholemeal/wholewheat flour
¼ teaspoon salt
100 g/½ cup caster/superfine sugar
¾ teaspoon bicarbonate of soda/ baking soda
435-g/15-oz. can crushed pineapple in its own juice
60 g/¼ cup apple sauce
120 ml/½ cup pineapple juice
60 ml/¼ cup coconut milk
1 teaspoon vanilla extract
1 teaspoon apple cider vinegar
handful of toasted coconut chips or dessicated coconut, to decorate

12-hole muffin pan, lightly greased with a little coconut oil or lined with baking parchment

Preheat the oven to 200°C (400°F) Gas 6.

In a large bowl, mix together the polenta/cornmeal, flour, salt, sugar and bicarbonate of soda/baking soda.

In a separate bowl, combine the crushed pineapple with its juice, apple sauce, pineapple juice, coconut milk, vanilla extract and vinegar.

Add the combined wet ingredients to the bowl of combined dry ingredients and gently mix together until you have a moist batter.

Using a spoon, fill each greased muffin hole with the mixture. Bake in the preheated oven for 30 minutes or until an inserted cocktail stick/toothpick comes out clean.

Allow to cool, then sprinkle a few toasted coconut chips on each one.

TIP

Try adding a large handful of blueberries or desiccated/ dried shredded coconut to the batter before baking.

You can also swap the pineapple juice for 60 ml/¼ cup lime juice and 60 ml/¼ cup pineapple juice, and decorate with a lime drizzle (1 lime, juiced, combined with 90 g/ 7 tablespoons granulated sugar) and a little lime zest.

These are also delicious served warm from the oven, sliced in half, buttered and drizzled with runny honey.

KŪLOLO

A traditional Hawaiian pudding, this looks like a dense loaf cake with a consistency similar to sticky syrup pudding crossed with malt loaf. Make sure you wear gloves when preparing taro and don't eat it raw as, prior to cooking, it can be an irritant.

SERVES 6

580 g/3 cups peeled and grated taro root (you could also use yam or sweet potato, though these will give slightly different results)

235 ml/1 cup coconut water

235 ml/1 cup coconut milk

75 g/3 oz. fresh coconut, finely grated

150 g/¾ cup brown sugar

900-g/2-lb loaf pan, greased with a little coconut oil, then lined with foil and greased again

Preheat the oven to 190°C (375°F) Gas 5.

In a food processor, blitz the grated taro with the coconut water and coconut milk. Add the grated coconut and blitz again. Stir through the sugar thoroughly, ensuring there are no lumps of sugar and that the mixture is well combined. At this stage you should have a thick, textured paste, more like a batter than a dough. If the mixture is too dry, stir in a little more coconut milk until you have the right consistency.

Spoon into the prepared loaf pan and cover with greased foil. Bake in the preheated oven for 2 hours. For a more authentic result, steam the pudding in a steamer or bain-marie (in the tin, covered with foil) for about 8 hours.

Allow to cool completely (ideally overnight), slice and enjoy on its own or toasted, with a scoop of Piña Colada Sherbet (see below).

PIÑA COLADA SHERBET

Fruity yet creamy, this is a cross between ice cream and sorbet. Our Piña Colada version is a refreshing and indulgent way to treat yourself to something sweet but light. It can be made days in advance and is sure to please guests of all ages.

SERVES 6–8

200 g/1 cup caster/superfine sugar

120 ml/½ cup pineapple juice

1 tablespoon grated lemon zest

1 tablespoon freshly squeezed lemon juice

250 ml/1 cup plus 1 tablespoon coconut milk

300 ml/1¼ cups milk

1 teaspoon vanilla extract

Mix all the ingredients together in a bowl. Pour into a freezerproof container, cover with a lid and freeze for an hour or so, until the top has frozen over.

Put the mixture back into a mixing bowl and beat with a wooden spoon or blend in a blender on a low setting until creamy and free from ice crystals. Return to the freezerproof container, cover and freeze for another 2 hours before repeating the above step.

Freeze fully and serve.

TIP

Serve in ice-cream cones decorated with some toasted coconut chips. For a more grown up version, substitute 75 ml/5 tablespoons coconut milk for Malibu rum.

THE POKE JOURNEY
& THE AVOCADO EFFECT

Los Angeles is a special place for me as it's always the city I go through when heading up to Santa Barbara, off to Hawai'i, or inland to places like Yosemite.

By the very nature of passing through it quickly, I usually consider the fast food culture accessible mainly by car as the 'true LA experience'. Favourite places have been Mexican taco joints on the beach, blender and smoothie shops, and of course In-n-Out Burger. Lately, the niche, neighbourhood-style taquerias in Santa Monica have been my choice for that quick LA Mex fix, but alongside these unique So-Cal Mexican experiences has been the sudden influx of poke shops in Santa Monica and West-side Los Angeles. These have taken LA by storm and are spreading all over the city. Angelenos apparently cannot get enough poke. This poke is in a style quite developed from the original Hawaiian supermarket variety. The appeal here is a healthy, varied combination of ingredients that stretches the Hawaiian roots to their limit.

Despite being based predominantly in beach communities and playing off the casual 'surfer dude' connotations, poke in LA has a sophisticated clientele of trendy types, Hollywood wannabes, workout addicts and ladies looking for that lunch with minimal carbs. They have taken customizing your poke combinations in the 'build your own bowl' concept to extreme levels. It's not unusual to see everything from Japanese-style pickles, sprouts, kale, and broccoli for the veggies, and several types of flavoured and coloured rice. Add to this the inevitable So-Cal Mexican undertones to be found in the bowl alternatives, including burritos, quesadillas and tacos, and you should have some idea of what Los Angeles has done with poke.

Above all else, one ingredient that screams Southern California features in the LA mindset of what 'needs' to be included in one's poke. This is the avocado. Previously featured in pretty much all So-Cal Mexican cooking alongside health food specials that featured the avocado mashed on thinly sliced rye, it is now front and centre in poke.

My California slant on this ingredient could be summed up by a little aside on JC, one of my buddies in Santa Barbara who I've known since we were little kids. Clean eating wasn't universally known or understood, but if anyone epitomized this concept and possibly took it to extremes, it was JC. For instance, drinking anything from a bottle required it to be glass rather than plastic. Avocados

Left to right: The Santa Monica pier next to the beach in California; Surfers walking on the shoreline on Venice beach, California; Local organic produce stall in Hawai'i; In-n-Out Burger, Hollywood.

feature big time with JC as he lives on a ranch surrounded by them. He not only eats them, but squishes them up for skin lotions that he slathers all over, and uses as his favoured hair conditioner. Just as Laplanders have about 100 words for snow, JC has many words to describe the variety, shape, condition, colour and, most importantly, taste of an avocado.

Avocados were not, however, at the forefront of JC's mind when it came to food. After spending most of the day surfing, swimming or spear-fishing, fish or seafood were the principal targets. One of his favourite pursuits was the little lobsters inhabiting the rocks under the kelp beds. After a session on our boards, JC would say 'I'm going to look around these rocks, there's bound to be lobsters'. He would bring back a little collection of very much live lobsters and would eat the tails raw, right there on the beach, by snapping them in half, and throwing the heads back in the sea (for the benefit of the eco-system). If there was a lemon tree nearby for a touch of finesse, then all the better.

If we actually prepared anything with more elaboration, say, if we were having dinner in a friend's backyard, then the combinations would be assembled with the ever-present corn tortilla or chips and Tapatio hot sauce. Lobsters and fish would be lightly ceviched and eaten straight out of the bowl with local La Tolteca corn tortilla chips. Naturally, avocados would never be very far away, either sliced or made into guacamole, and those local lemons would always feature. If JC had anything to do with it, he would bring a big bag of them.

As everyone knows, Los Angeles culture is not confined simply to the city limits. It pretty much sets the tone for much of the west coast from Seattle all the way down to what is essentially an LA neighbourhood down in Cabo San Lucas in Baja California. Most of the poke you find around here is a derivation of what started in the LA West-side. There are some exceptions, such as Sam Choy's Poke to the Max in Seattle catering to Pacific Island tastes, but in general, poke has become an essential ingredient in the elusive sense of being in that LA lifestyle. Poke has now moved along with these So-Cal influences to other parts of the US, and other parts of the world. It has picked up other variations from Japanese sushi chefs and fish tartare specialists. No doubt it will continue to evolve as its popularity spreads further from its original versions back on those counters at the local supermarkets in Hawai'i.

AÇAÍ BOWL

Açaí, although found in the Amazon, is quickly becoming a Hawaiian breakfast staple. It is an amazing super food, with the berries picked and immediately frozen to lock in the goodness. Açaí is seriously addictive – you have been warned...

MAKES 1 BOWL

100-g/3½-oz. pouch of açaí berries
50 g/⅓ cup frozen blueberries
120 ml/½ cup almond milk
handful of granola
handful of fresh raspberries
  and fresh blueberries
sprinkle of goji berries
sprinkle of cacao nibs
1 tablespoon toasted coconut
agave syrup (optional)

Break up the açaí berries in the pouch, then put them into a blender with the frozen blueberries and almond milk and blend. It should be the consistency of ice cream – if it needs loosening, add more almond milk.

Add it to your serving bowl, then get artistic. Add the granola, gojis, cacao nibs and toasted coconut on one half the bowl and add the fresh fruit decoratively in the middle in a line. Drizzle agave syrup over the berries so it gives them a nice shine, if you like.

TIP
Add whatever suits your fancy: chia seeds, mango, kiwi or muesli. Or blend with an extra 150 ml/⅔ cup fruit juice, coconut water or almond milk to enjoy as a smoothie.

PITAYA LATTE

Pitaya (also known as dragon fruit) has become a dietary staple amongst health-conscious Islanders. A cactus fruit packed with Omega-3 and antioxidants, its fuchsia-coloured flesh makes it a popular, Insta-friendly alternative to açaí. Recent years have seen the rise of the 'Superfood Latte', and this pretty pink Pitaya Latte is easy on the eye, kind to your body and tasty like a comforting cup of heaven.

SERVES 1

235 ml/1 cup oat milk
½ tablespoon pitaya powder,
  plus extra for sprinkling
1 teaspoon coconut oil
1 teaspoon vanilla extract
1 teaspoon almond butter
coconut sugar or agave syrup,
  to taste

Warm the oat milk in a small saucepan.

Mix the pitaya powder with 1 teaspoon hot water, making sure it is properly dissolved.

Add the warm milk to a blender with all the other ingredients, including the dissolved pitaya powder, and blend until frothy.

Pour into a mug and serve immediately. Top with a little sprinkle of pitaya powder for an extra splash of colour.

LYCHEE LEMONADE

The lychee tree was first introduced to Hawai'i in the late 1800s. Although its fruit isn't grown there commercially, the trees can still be found in many backyards. This lychee version of lemonade is a nice option if you're entertaining as it has an exotic, fragrant, slightly sophisticated air while retaining the fun, home-made element of old-fashioned lemonade.

SERVES 4

16–20 ripe lychees
freshly squeezed juice of 3 lemons
granulated sugar, to taste (optional,
  depending on the sweetness of the
  lychees)
handful of ice (optional)
1 litre/1 quart water, chilled
fresh mint sprigs, to decorate
  (optional)
pared/grated lemon zest, to decorate
  (optional)

Peel and deseed the lychees. Add the flesh to a blender and mix to make a smooth purée. Squeeze in the lemon juice. Taste the purée and add a little sugar to sweeten if necessary.

Put the fruit purée into a water jug/pitcher and add ice according to personal preference. Top up with the chilled water, stirring until well blended. Top with a few mint sprigs and some lemon zest for decoration, if you like, and enjoy.

TIP

For a more grown up summer cocktail, try adding some gin, vodka or rum! Adjust the water quantities depending on how concentrated you like your lemonade.

ISLAND DAISY

Our version of the classic Margarita features gin instead of tequila. It takes the drink back to the original version that was called a Daisy. We've kept things old school, with triple sec for the citrusy element, and topping up with fizzy water.

SERVES 4

120 ml/½ cup gin – a classic London Dry Gin
    is best, such as Sipsmith
60 ml/¼ cup triple sec
60 ml/¼ cup freshly squeezed lime juice
2 teaspoons agave syrup
ice cubes
fizzy water – Badoit extra fizzy is the best option
lime wedges, to garnish

Pre-chill the serving glasses in the freezer.

Combine the gin, triple sec, lime juice and agave syrup in a cocktail shaker. Shake to mix. Add ice cubes to the chilled glasses, pour in equal measures of the mixture, top up with fizzy water and garnish each glass with a lime wedge. (The amount of fizzy water to pour in is up to you – we suggest it's no more than a third of the total drink.)

FRESH PINEAPPLE MARGARITA

Not an attempt to Hawaiian-ize the Margarita, but a genuine, frothy and fruity tasting version. Try to use a super-sweet pineapple to get things off in the right direction and follow up with a reasonable silver tequila. This is also known as Pineapple Fluff.

SERVES 4

½ fresh pineapple, chilled
freshly squeezed juice of 2 limes
120 ml/½ cup Cointreau or triple sec
235 ml/1 cup silver tequila
ice cubes
agave syrup, to taste (optional)
pineapple wedges, to decorate

Pre-chill the serving glasses in the freezer.

Cut the half pineapple into four wedges lengthways. Run the knife along the peel of each wedge to remove, then cut the pineapple into chunks.

Put the pineapple, lime juice, Cointreau or triple sec, and tequila in a blender with a few ice cubes and whizz up to a smooth, frothy mix. Add a little agave syrup if it needs some sweetening. Pour immediately into the chilled glasses and garnish with a wedge of pineapple on the rims.

MANGO DAIQUIRI

Beachside Baja California in a glass.

SERVES 4

6 large mangoes, or equivalent amount
  of frozen mango
2 litres ice
350 ml/1½ cups light rum
granulated sugar, to taste

Pre-chill the serving glasses in the freezer.

If using fresh mangoes, peel and stone the mangoes, then slice. Put into a blender with an equal volume of ice and whizz until you have a smooth purée. Add the rum, and sugar to taste, pulse again. Pour immediately into the chilled glasses.

If using frozen mango, put it straight into the blender with half the volume of ice. Whizz until you have a smooth purée. Add the rum, and sugar to taste, pulse again. Pour immediately into the chilled glasses.

YUZU G & T

The classic cocktail at our Broadgate Circle shop.

SERVES 2

1 tablespoon yuzu powder
1 tablespoon caster/superfine sugar
2 teaspoons yuzu juice
2 teaspoons agave syrup
2 measures (50 ml/1¾ oz.) gin
200-ml/7-oz. bottle Indian tonic water
  – we like Fever-Tree
ice

HIBISCUS G & T

A Hawaiian take on an English classic.

SERVES 2

2 tablespoons hibiscus syrup – home-made
  (see below) or store bought
2 measures (50 ml/2 oz.) gin
200 ml/7 oz. bottle Indian tonic water
  – we prefer Fever-Tree
ice
2 edible fresh hibiscus flowers, to garnish

FOR THE HIBISCUS SYRUP
50 g/¼ cup white sugar
40 g/½ cup edible fresh hibiscus flowers
140 g/½ cup runny honey

To make the hibiscus syrup, in a small pan, bring the sugar and 235 ml/1 cup water to the boil. When it has just reached the boil, turn off the heat and add the hibiscus flowers. Leave to steep for 30 minutes. Add the honey and cool completely. Strain into a jar, seal and refrigerate. Use within a week. (Alternatively, use ready-made hibiscus syrup.)

To make the drinks, put a tablespoon of hibiscus syrup into each glass, add the gin and stir with tonic and ice. Garnish each with an edible hibiscus flower.

Pre-chill the serving glasses in the freezer.

Turn the glasses upside down on a plate with some water to moisten the rims. Combine the yuzu powder and sugar on another plate. Place the glass rims on the plate to lightly coat.

In these glasses, stir together the yuzu juice and agave syrup, add some ice and a measure of gin to each glass. Top up with tonic water and stir.

BLENDERS & SMOOTHIES

MELEMELE

*All the yellows. A super cleansing
and restorative juice.*

SERVES 2

1 yellow (bell) pepper
2 yellow carrots
2 yellow apples, such as Golden Delicious,
    Opal, Yellow Golden, etc.
thumb-sized piece of fresh ginger

Simply blitz all the ingredients together
in a blender.

GLOW JUICE

*Alkalinize with this juice, that is also
very low in sugar. Use a juice extractor.*

SERVES 2

1 bunch of celery, stalks only
1 cucumber
1 apple
1 tablespoon apple cider vinegar
thumb-sized piece of fresh ginger

Simply put all the ingredients into a juicer
and blitz.

BLUE HAWAI'I

*Super-rich and super-good.
Use a blender for this one.*

SERVES 2

¼ fresh pineapple, peeled and cored
150 ml/⅔ cup coconut water
flesh from ¼ fresh coconut
large handful of blueberries
1 teaspoon Blue Majik

Blend everything together until the
coconut flesh is fine and smooth.

PALM SPRINGS DATE SHAKE

*Imagine you're lying by a pool in Palm
Springs! An iconic drink from the date-
growing Coachella Valley in California.*

SERVES 2

70 g/½ cup stoned dates, such
    as Deglet Noor, Medjool, etc.
pinch of ground cinnamon
pinch of salt
300 ml/1¼ cups almond or coconut milk
8 tablespoons/1 cup vanilla ice cream
½ cup ice cubes

Rehydrate the dates a little by placing them
in a small bowl with a glass of hot water. Leave
to soak for 15 minutes.
    Put the dates and their soaking liquid in a blender
with the cinnamon, salt and milk and whizz until the
dates are reduced to a coarse pulp. Add the ice cream
and ice and blend until very smooth.

INDEX

ACKNOWLEDGEMENTS

First of all, I would not be here without the support of my amazing team at Island Poké. Thanks guys.

A special thank you must be made to Lauren Blissett, our in-house native Hawaiian who greatly helped sourcing and compiling those very special local recipes among her extended family – including her granny, aunties and friends on the islands. She tirelessly researched, met the deadlines and came up with some great ideas.

Thank you to Lauren's mother, Julie, Grandmother, Aunty Terese, Aunty Jo, Aunty Ann, Aunty Nohea, Dave Wong, Kaiwahine and Ikaika for all your tips and for inspiring us with your cultural knowledge and cooking skills! Mahalo piha.

Thanks to Dave Burt, Joel Smedley and Lauren for your photographic contributions.

A big thank you to the Hawaiian people who have inspired me so much.

A word needs to be said about the influence of my friends in both California and Hawai'i. I would not have been able to switch into a west-coast mindset coming from my usual English school culture without their contribution and friendship. This goes out particularly to John 'JC' Clark for his nativeness, freethinking and passion for the avocado, Scott 'Scotty' Korchinski for keeping me aware of the Poké developments in LA, Mark Outwater for teaching me the skill of fishing in the Pacific, and John 'Johnno' Outwater for sharing a Hansens in the hot tub after pushing my surfing abilities to the limit and endless try tip BBQs. I am especially grateful for the photos he provided for the book. John's twin passions for surfing and photography take him regularly back to Hawai'i where he can truly indulge.

Finally, thanks to Dad, for continued support through thick and thin.

PICTURE CREDITS

All photography by Mowie Kay apart from pages:

4–5 M Swiet Productions/Getty Images; 7 Dave Burt and Joel Smedley; 10–11 William Lingwood/Ryland Peters & Small; 14 Nat Farbman/The LIFE Picture Collection/Getty Images; 18 Miki Cabatbat/EyeEm/Getty Images; 22–23 Brent Olsons/Getty Images; 24l M.M. Sweet/Getty Images; 24c International Game Fish Association via Getty Images; 24r Karen Kasmauski/Getty Images; 25l David Hiser/Getty Images; 25r John Humble/Getty Images; 40 ilbusca/iStock; 44–45 SuperStock/Getty Images; 49 ilbusca/iStock; 52–53 Ed Freeman/Getty Images; 54l Westend61/Getty Images; 54c Steve Proehl/Getty Images; 54r joSon/Getty; 55l George Silk/The LIFE Picture Collection/Getty Images; 55r Sergi Reboredo/VW PICS/UIG via Getty Images; 56 Allan Seiden/Getty Images; 60 Underwood Archives/Getty Images; 67 overkoffeined/Shutterstock.com; 71 Pingebat/iStock; 74–75 Vince Cavataio/Getty Images; 79 MoreVector/Shutterstock.com; 80 Bettmann/Getty Images; 82–83 Richard A Cooke Iii./Getty Images; 84l Jamie Gril/Getty Images; 84r Brandon Tabiolo/Getty Images; 85l Kicka Witte/Getty Images; 88 Eliot Elisofon//Time Life Pictures/Getty Images; 92 Frank Scherschel/Time Life Pictures/Getty Images; 96 & 99 ilbusca/iStock; 104–105 Dana Edmunds/Design Pics/Getty Images; 109 Authenticated News/Archive Photos/Getty Images; 114l WIN-Initiative/Getty Images; 114c Jeffrey Greenberg/UIG via Getty Images; 114r Douglas Peebles/Getty Images; 115r Lauren Blissett 119 bauhaus1000/iStock; 126–127 Matt Anderson Photography/Getty Images; Damien Gavios/EyeEm/Getty Images; 147 Paul Popper/Popperfoto/Getty Images; 151 Channarong Pherngjanda/Shutterstock.com; 160–161 Brent Olsons/Getty Images; 162l Jason Merritt/FilmMagic for Nickelodeon Television; 162r Joe Kohen/Getty Images; 163l Andrea Sperling/Getty Images; 163r Education Images/Citizens of the Planet/UIG via Getty Images; 165 Orlando/Getty Images.